CAMPAIGN 75

LORRAINE 1944

PATTON vs MANTEUFFEL

SERIES EDITOR: LEE JOHNSON

CAMPAIGN 75

LORRAINE 1944

PATTON vs MANTEUFFEL

WRITTEN BY
STEVEN J ZALOGA

ILLUSTRATED BY
TONY BRYAN

OSPREY
MILITARY

First published in Great Britain in 2000 by Osprey Publishing, Elms Court, Chapel Way, Botley, Oxford OX2 9LP, United Kingdom.
Email: info@ospreypublishing.com

ISBN 1 84176 089 7

Project Editor: Marcus Cowper
Editor: Judith Millidge
Design: Black Spot
Wargaming section: Arthur Harman
Cartography: The Map Studio
Colour bird's eye views: Paul Kime

Origination by Valhaven Ltd, Isleworth, UK
Printed in China through World Print Ltd

For a catalogue of all books published by Osprey Military, Automotive and Aviation please contact:

The Marketing Manager, Osprey Direct UK, PO Box 140, Wellingborough, Northants, NN8 4ZA, United Kingdom.
Tel. (0)1933 443863, Fax (0)1933 443849.
E-mail: info@ospreydirect.co.uk

The Marketing Manager, Osprey Direct USA, P.O. Box 130, Sterling Heights, MI 48311-0130, United States of America
Email: info@ospreydirectusa.com

Visit Osprey's website at:
http://www.ospreypublishing.com

Author's Note

The author would like to thank the staff of the US Army's Military History Institute at the Army War College at Carlisle Barracks, PA, for their kind assistance in the preparation of this book. Thanks also go to Col. David Glantz (Retired) who was kind enough to provide copies of many unit histories and other documents from his library. The author would also like to thank Thomas Jentz for his assistance in providing detailed data on German tank strengths and losses in Lorraine, based on his archival research. Thanks also go to David Isby for providing aerial photos of the battlefield. The photos in this book are primarily from the US Army's Signal Corps collections located formerly at the Pentagon and the Defense Audio-Visual Agency at Anacostia Navy Yard, and now at the US National Archives in College Park, MD. Other Signal Corps photos were located at the special collections branch of the Military History Institute, and the German photos are primarily from the captured German photos collections of the US National Archives. The photographs of the battlefields in Lorraine were taken by the author in September 1999, 55 years after the actual fighting.

Artist's Note

KEY TO MILITARY SYMBOLS

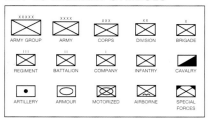

PAGE 2: **An M4 crosses the Moselle on a treadway bridge, while in the background, the remains of another destroyed bridge can be seen. (US Army)**

PAGE 3: **Private Kenneth Boyer, a tanker of the HQ company of 37th Tank Bn. on board his M4 (105mm) assault gun on 26 September 1944 during the Arracourt fighting.**

CONTENTS

THE STRATEGIC SITUATION

In September 1944, Hitler sensed the opportunity to deal the Allies a crushing blow. Patton's Third Army was spearheading the Allied advance eastward, and as his forces attacked into Lorraine, they seemed on the verge of penetrating the Westwall defenses into Germany itself. However, Patton's right flank was exposed while the US 6th Army Group moved northward along the Swiss frontier, having landed a month earlier in southern France. So by massing several of the newly formed Panzer brigades, Hitler prepared for a major armored counteroffensive in Lorraine. His aim was to encircle and destroy Patton's forces. To lead this audacious attack and head up the Fifth Panzer Army, he chose one of his youngest and most aggressive tank commanders, Gen. Hasso von Manteuffel. This would be the largest German panzer counterattack on the Western Front and one of the largest tank versus tank battles fought by the US Army in World War II. The tank battles in Lorraine in September 1944 are the focus of this book.

Alsace-Lorraine had been a warpath between France and Germany for centuries: taken by Germany in the wake of the 1870 Franco-Prussian War, it was recovered by France after 1918 and then reabsorbed into

During August, Patton's Third Army raced across France as the Wehrmacht retreated in disorder. Here, on 21 August 1944, an M4 tank of the 8th Tank Bn., 4th Armd. Div. fires on German troops across the Marne River, trying to destroy one of its bridges. The 4th Armd. Div. was usually Patton's spearhead, and would play the central role in the September tank fighting in Lorraine. (US Army)

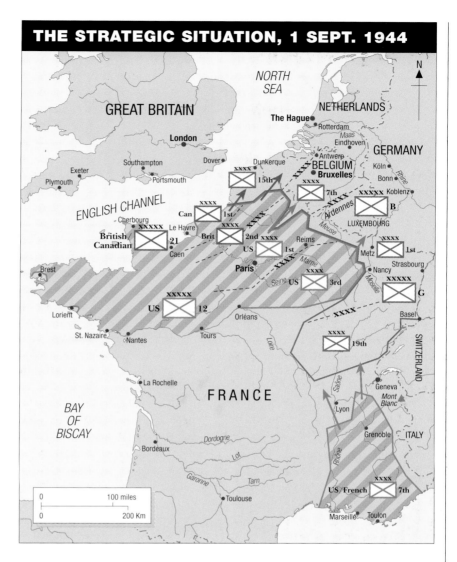

Germany after 1940. As a traditional invasion route between the two countries, the area has also been fortified over the centuries with great fortress cities such as Metz. The "Charmes Gap" figured in French war plans in 1914, and the nearby Verdun forts were the center of the fighting in 1916. The French side of Lorraine was the site of portions of the Maginot Line, mirrored on the German frontier by the Westwall which was also called the Siegfried Line.

At the beginning of September 1944, the Allies were optimistic the war might soon be won. In August, German forces in northern France had been encircled and smashed in the Falaise Gap. German casualties had exceeded 300,000 killed and captured, and a further 200,000 had been trapped in the Atlantic ports and Channel Islands. For nearly a month, the Allied armies had advanced with little opposition, surging past Paris and into Belgium. In the east, the German forces had suffered an equally shattering setback with the destruction of Army Group Center in Byelorussia as a result of the Red Army's Operation Bagration. A subsequent offensive through Ukraine had pushed the German forces

completely out of the Soviet Union and into central Poland along the Vistula River. While the central region of the front had stabilized by the beginning of August, the Red Army had poured into the Balkans. Germany's eastern allies – Finland, Romania, Hungary, and Bulgaria – were on the verge of switching sides, and Germany's main source of oil in the Romanian fields near Ploesti was soon to be lost. On 20 July 1944, German officers attempted to assassinate Hitler, and some believed that this signaled the beginning of a German collapse, similar to that experienced by the German Army in the autumn of 1918.

The Anglo-American forces under Gen. Dwight Eisenhower comprised three main elements. Gen. Bernard Montgomery's 21st Army Group on the left flank was advancing from the regions of Dieppe and Amiens towards Flanders. The 21st Army Group consisted of the First Canadian Army, on the extreme left, and the Second British Army to its right. The main American element was Gen. Omar Bradley's 12th Army Group, consisting of Hodges' First Army, moving to the north-east into central Belgium, and Gen. George S. Patton's Third Army moving through the Argonne into Lorraine. In addition, Gen. Jacob Devers' 6th Army Group, consisting of the US Seventh Army and the French First Army, had landed in southern France and was advancing northward along the Swiss border towards the Belfort Gap.

German forces in France lost most of their armored equipment in the Normandy campaign and the ensuing envelopment at Falaise. Of the 1,890 tanks and assault guns available on D-Day, about 1,700 were lost. This is a salvage yard in Travières, France, on 4 September 1944, showing some of the captured equipment. In the foreground are two tank destroyers based on captured French chassis, while to the right are three Panther tanks. (US Army)

OPPOSING PLANS

GERMAN PLANS

From the German perspective, the strategic situation was an unrelieved disaster. The Wehrmacht was in headlong retreat from France, and the immediate tasks were to reconstitute German forces in the west and hold back the Allied forces while defenses in depth were strengthened along the Westwall. In the wake of the attempted military coup in July, Adolf Hitler was extremely suspicious of German military leaders, and he imposed an even tighter control on all military operations down to the tactical level. Hitler remained contemptuous of the Anglo-American armies, and was convinced that bold operations could derail the Allied advance. In spite of the utter failure of his panzer counteroffensive at Mortain a month earlier, Hitler was entranced with the concept of cutting off and destroying the lead elements of the Anglo-American forces. He expected that his panzer forces could win great encirclement battles in the west as they so often had on the Eastern Front. Not surprisingly, he selected veterans from the Eastern Front to conduct his offensive in Lorraine.

At the beginning of September, German forces in the west were under the command of Generalfeldmarschall Gerd von Rundstedt. These included Generalfeldmarschall Walter Model's Army Group B, with four armies from the North Sea to the area around Nancy, and the much smaller Army Group G, under Generaloberst Johannes Blaskowitz, with only a single army covering from Nancy southward to the Swiss frontier.

Hitler believed that a violent panzer attack against Patton's Third Army was both the most necessary and the most promising option. Patton's Third Army had advanced the furthest east, and its momentum towards the Saar suggested that it would be the first Allied force to enter Germany. Besides blunting this threatening advance, a panzer counterattack towards Reims would have the added benefit of preventing the link-up between Devers' 6th Army Group advancing from southern France and Bradley's 12th Army Group in northern France. On 3 September 1944, Hitler instructed Rundstedt to begin planning this attack. Under Hitler's initial plan, the attack would be carried out by the 3rd, 15th, and 17th SS Panzer Grenadier Divisions, the new Panzer Brigades 111, 112, and 113, and with later reinforcements from the Panzer Lehr Division, 11th and 21st Panzer Divisions and the new Panzer Brigades 106, 107, and 108. The Fifth Panzer Army headquarters would be shifted from Belgium to Alsace-Lorraine to control the panzer counteroffensive. On 5 September 1944, the newly appointed commander of Fifth Panzer Army, Gen. Hasso von Manteuffel, flew in straight from the fighting on the Eastern Front to be

personally briefed by Hitler on the objectives of the counteroffensive. The date of the counterattack was initially set for 12 September 1944, but events soon overtook these plans.

ALLIED PLANS

The dilemma facing Allied planners in September 1944 was very different. Towards the end of August 1944, many Allied military leaders had begun to wonder whether the Germans might completely collapse, as they had done in 1918. Under such circumstances, a continuing string of bold advances could best take advantage of the German plight. Yet there remained the nagging doubt that the Germans might prove resilient and that their resistance might stiffen as the prewar German frontier was attacked.

The advance through France in August 1944 had seen the Allied forces achieve far more than was originally planned: they had expected to be on the Seine River in early September when in fact they were now 150 miles beyond. Indeed, Patton's Third Army was at the phase line expected for April 1945. The most immediate consequence of the unexpectedly speedy advance was that the Allied forces were beginning to experience serious logistical difficulties. Supplies landed on the Normandy beaches had to be trucked forward, since the French railroad network had been shattered by pre-invasion bombing. Shortages in fuel and ammunition would become a critical determinant of combat capabilities in the autumn of 1944. Ideally, a port closer to the front was needed. The most likely candidate was Antwerp, which was large enough to handle the necessary volume of supplies. This was in the British sector, and Montgomery's 21st Army Group was given the vital assignment of securing it.

Beyond the short-term need to improve the supply situation before pressing on into Germany, there remained controversy over how best to conduct operations. In May 1944, the SHAEF (Supreme Headquarters Allied Expeditionary Force) had completed studies which recommended a broad front advance with two main axes of attack. The main drive would take place through Belgium, north of the Ardennes forest, then swing behind the Rhine River to eliminate Germany's industrial heart in the Ruhr. This would involve Mongomery's 21st Army Group and the US First Army. The secondary axis of attack would be through Lorraine towards Frankfurt, to take the Saar industrial region and win bridgeheads over the Rhine into central Germany. This would involve Patton's Third Army and the 6th Army Group.

The supply problems of September 1944 led to questions about these plans, especially from the commander of the British forces, Gen. Bernard Montgomery. In early September, Montgomery argued that the lack of sufficient supplies would make a broad front attack impossible. Instead, he urged that the resources be directed to his 21st Army Group, which could make a bold thrust through the Netherlands. Montgomery contended that Germany was on the brink of defeat and that his forces could race to Berlin, bringing about a swift end of the war. As September progressed and German resistance began to stiffen, Montgomery stuck with his single-thrust strategy, arguing that it was still the best alternative to close on the Ruhr and end the war through industrial strangulation. Underlying this debate was an unstated recognition that Britain was losing its once-dominant position in the Allied coalition. The British Army had committed all of its ground forces, and as the war continued, the US Army would play an increasingly important role in the fighting. Montgomery's championing of British leadership in the assault on Germany was an attempt to push off his inevitable loss of influence as the British forces shrank as a proportion of the Allied armies.

Montgomery's position was vehemently contested by US Army leaders, especially by his American counterpart, Gen. Omar Bradley. The US Army commanders had lost confidence in Montgomery following his conduct in the prolonged armored offensives to take Caen during the Normandy campaign, and they were skeptical of his ability to achieve the rapid offensive he proposed. The American leadership was suspicious of Montgomery's motives, feeling that he was prompted more by his desire for British forces to play the predominant role in the European campaign than by realistic tactical advantage. Bradley wanted to continue Patton's advance through Lorraine, in the hope of being able to seize Rhine crossings towards Frankfurt should German resistance continue to be weak. Montgomery's plan would force Patton's Third Army to halt before breaching the Moselle River line and before joining up with Devers' 6th Army Group.

The supreme Allied commander, Gen. Dwight Eisenhower, attempted to mediate, with little appreciation from either side. Montgomery was openly contemptuous of Eisenhower's ability as a field commander, while Bradley felt that he was overly solicitous to Montgomery's exorbitant demands. The importance of seizing Antwerp led to Eisenhower granting Montgomery priority in the allotment of supplies on 4 September, but arguments continued through early September over how much priority 21st Army Group would in fact receive. The key issue remained the Allies' perception of the condition of the German forces. Was the Wehrmacht on the brink of collapse, or was it on the brink of recovery? If on the verge of collapse, then bold ventures were worth the risk, but if on the verge of recovery, then steps were needed to ensure that the Allied armies would be ready to conduct well-prepared operations into Germany in the ensuing months. The Allies were reaching the end of the logistical possibilities of the Normandy harbors, and the supply question needed attention.

On 3 September 1944, Montgomery first mentioned to Bradley plans for a proposed operation called Market-Garden, with an aim to seize a bridgehead over the Rhine with airborne forces at Arnhem as the first stage of a northern Ruhr envelopment. Bradley was opposed to the plan, feeling that it was impractical and too risky. In a cable to Eisenhower on 4 September, Montgomery continued to urge "a powerful and full-blooded thrust towards Berlin." The issue finally came to a head at a 10 September meeting. Montgomery again demanded a thrust on Berlin, but it became evident that Eisenhower would not consider any such operation until the port of Antwerp was functioning. By mid-September, Eisenhower had lost his late-August optimism about Germany's imminent collapse and was becoming more convinced that the Germans were rallying. Montgomery then presented his daring Market-Garden plan. Eisenhower approved Market-Garden as a less fanciful and less disruptive alternative to the Berlin adventure.

Eisenhower's decision to approve Market-Garden shaped the subsequent conduct of Allied operations in September. The broad front strategy had not been given up, but realistically the supply problem would limit the amount of offensive operations the Allies could conduct. Eisenhower gave priority to the northern thrust, including both the 21st Army Group's Market-Garden operation and a supporting drive by the US First Army in Belgium to protect the British right flank. Patton's advance in Lorraine was not yet frozen, but its potential was severely circumscribed by the likelihood of supply cut-offs. The debate over the Berlin dagger-thrust and Market-Garden had also distracted the Allied leaders from concentrating on the need to secure Antwerp by clearing the Scheldt estuary. Montgomery's preoccupation with offensive operations led to serious delays in devoting resources to the Scheldt, and as a result, Antwerp was not ready to begin receiving supplies until the

Commander of the Fifth Panzer Army, General der Panzertruppe Hasso von Manteuffel, on the left, confers with the Army Group A commander, Gen. Walter Model (right) and the inspector of the panzer force on the Western Front, Gen. Lt. Horst Stumpff (center). (US Army MHI)

end of November 1944. This would prove to be one of the most critical Allied blunders of the autumn campaign.

The Germans did not expect so bold a venture as Market-Garden from the Allies, especially not from so cautious a commander as Montgomery. As a result of both sides' misperceptions of the other's strategic intentions, the contest between Patton's Third Army and Manteuffel's Fifth Panzer Army was more equal than it otherwise might have been. The German forces in Lorraine received priority in supplies and equipment because of Hitler's planned panzer offensive, while their American opponents were being constrained in their operations by supply limits. Patton's forces in Lorraine still enjoyed some significant firepower advantages over the Wehrmacht, but the unusually rainy weather in September restricted the amount of air support that was possible. The Germans enjoyed the advantage of the formidable defensive possibilities presented by the Metz fortified area, as well as the natural defenses of the Moselle valley.

OPPOSING COMMANDERS

GERMAN COMMANDERS

Adolf Hitler

While the main focus of this assessment is on the tactical commanders, it is impossible to detail the German side without considering Adolf Hitler, who had played an unusually active role in directing German military operations even before the failed military coup of 20 July 1944. After the unsuccessful assassination attempt, Hitler became even more suspicious of the commitment of the German generals to the war, and he insisted that the Wehrmacht "stand and hold" every inch of territory, thereby robbing the commanders of their tactical flexibility. Hitler's suspicions led to an extremely high degree of centralization, with commanders having to obtain permission from higher headquarters for any significant tactical decision. Senior generals were not trusted, and there was considerable turmoil in the upper ranks of the Wehrmacht as Hitler frequently replaced commanders. A large portion of the senior officers taking part in the Lorraine fighting in 1944 were brought in from the Eastern Front, as Hitler regarded them as less defeatist.

Wilhelm Keitel

The supreme German command nominally rested in the hands of the OKW (Oberkommando der Wehrmacht), headed by Generalfeldmarschall Wilhelm Keitel. Although the power of the OKW was circumscribed by Hitler's paranoia, it still retained an important function, since it could shape the Führer's views of the battle, and all subordinate commanders had to reach Hitler through the OKW structure.

Gerd von Rundstedt

SHAEF's German counterpart was the OB West (Oberbefehlshaber West), headed by Generalfeldmarschall Gerd von Rundstedt. He took over command of the Western Front on 1 September 1944, having given up the post in June 1944 after a confrontation with Hitler over the response to the Normandy invasion. Rundstedt remained the last of the undefeated German field marshals, with the stunning victories of 1939-40 to his credit, but his powers that September were severely restricted by Hitler and the OKW; and he later complained that he really only commanded the guards at his headquarters. Rundstedt had been brought back to act as a symbol of stability and to inspire confidence after the summer disasters.

Walter Model

Army Group B was commanded by Generalfeldmarschall Walter Model, who had been in charge of the entire Western Front until the OB West headquarters was reinstituted on 1 September 1944. Although Army Group B commanded most of the forces in Lorraine at the beginning of

September, a reorganization on 8 September shifted First Army to the neighboring Army Group G. Model was a favorite of Hitler – a brash, young officer better known as a trouble-shooter who could protect German fortunes in the face of staggering defeat than for his skills in conducting successful offensive operations.

The commander of Army Group G, Generaloberst Johannes Blaskowitz. (USNA)

Johannes Blaskowitz

Army Group G, near Nancy, was the centerpoint of the subsequent Lorraine panzer offensive. Army Group G had originally been organized to manage the German defense of southern France. Generaloberst Johannes Blaskowitz was a traditional German commander, more in the mold of Rundstedt than Model. East Prussian and non-political, he had commanded Eighth Army since October 1940 and had spent most of the war in command of First Army occupying France. At Rundstedt's insistence, Blaskowitz had been assigned command of Army Group G on 10 May 1944. Blaskowitz developed the reputation as an excellent organizer and capable commander, and the well-executed withdrawal of Army Group G from the Bay of Biscay and southern France to the Nancy sector was widely regarded as further evidence of his professional ability. Blaskowitz was unpopular at OKW due to his lack of enthusiasm for the Nazi regime, and was especially unpopular with the SS. A religious man, he had protested against SS atrocities in the Polish campaign in 1939 and ran into trouble again in early September 1944, when he queried Himmler's order for the creation of a defensive line behind his sector in the Nancy-Belfort area that was not under his control. His lack of interest in politics shielded him from the repercussions of the July military coup, and he retained the support of Rundstedt.

The commander of the German First Army, General der Panzertruppe Otto von Knobelsdorff. (US Army MHI)

Otto von Knobelsdorff

As of 8 September 1944, Army Group G consisted of the First Army and the Nineteenth Army. The First Army was commanded by General der Panzertruppe Otto von Knobelsdorff who had taken over after the army's retreat across France earlier in the summer. Knobelsdorff had distinguished himself as a panzer corps commander in the attempts to relieve Stalingrad. He was personally appointed by Hitler because of his bravery and unflinching optimism. Senior commanders felt that his tactical skills were unimpressive, and he was in poor physical shape after grueling service on the Eastern Front.

Friedrich Weise

The Nineteenth Army commander was General Friedrich Weise, who had been an infantry officer in World War I and, after serving in the police in the Weimar Republic, had returned to the army in 1935. Weise had advanced to divisional command in the autumn of 1942 and corps command a year later. He had been assigned to army command in France in June 1944, and his conduct of the retreat from southern France had acquainted him with the different battle style of the Western Front. He was a capable if unexceptional commander.

Hasso von Manteuffel

The most prominent tactical commander in the Lorraine fighting in September 1944 was General der Panzertruppe Hasso von Manteuffel,

The commander of the 47th Panzer Corps, General der Panzertruppen Heinrich Freiherr von Luttwitz. (US Army MHI)

another brash young officer, whose bravery and tactical skills had attracted Hitler's personal attention. Manteuffel had served as a cavalry officer in World War I, including duty at Verdun. He had remained a junior cavalry officer in the army after the war, switching to the new panzer branch in 1934. He had commanded an infantry battalion in Rommel's 7th Panzer Division in France in 1940, and had taken over regimental command in October 1941, during the fighting in the Soviet Union. He had been awarded the Knight's Cross for his action in seizing a bridgehead during the Moscow fighting in November 1941. Manteuffel had commanded a brigade in the North Africa campaign and while still a colonel formed an improvised division in Tunisia. (General von Arnim described him as one of his best divisional commanders in Tunisia.) Hitler had personally assigned him to command the 7th Panzer Division in June 1943 and transferred him to lead the élite Grossdeutschland Panzer Grenadier Division later in the year after he had been decorated with the Oakleaf for the Knight's Cross. Manteuffel's battlefield reputation and personal contacts with Hitler had led to his steady advancement, and on 1 September 1944 he was called to the Führer's headquarters and ordered to take command of Fifth Panzer Army, leapfrogging the ranks to army commander in a single step and bypassing the usual stage as a panzer corps commander. Manteuffel did not have the training or experience for the position, and would be further handicapped by the awkward deployment of the Fifth Panzer Army in sectors of the First and Nineteenth Armies.

ALLIED COMMANDERS

Unlike the Wehrmacht in the autumn of 1944, the US Army command structure was decentralized. Although Eisenhower, as SHAEF commander, made broad strategic decisions, he was seldom involved in any decisions below army level. His involvement in the actual Lorraine campaign was mainly in connection with the running debate over broad versus narrow front, and the allocation of supplies. Almost without exception, the senior US Army leaders were West Point graduates, part of a small but distinguished group of officers who had weathered the arid interwar years in regular army service as mid-ranking officers, and many of whom were personally acquainted with one another through long years of service.

Omar Bradley

General Omar Bradley commanded the US First Army in Normandy, and after the addition of Patton's Third Army in August, was promoted to lead the 12th Army Group. Here he is seen visiting with an M4 tank crew of Co. B, 34th Tank Bn. in November 1944.

The commander of the 12th Army Group was Gen. Omar Bradley, a fellow graduate of the West Point Class of 1915 with Eisenhower. Also like Eisenhower, Bradley had seen no overseas combat posting in World War I, but had earned a reputation in the interwar years as a quiet, hard-working staff officer. In 1940 he had commanded the Infantry School and later led the 82nd and 28th Divisions in succession. In early 1943, Eisenhower had required a deputy to serve as a trouble-shooter in North Africa. This position was short-lived, as the poor performance of the II Corps at Kasserine Pass had led to the relief of the corps commander and his replacement by Gen. George S. Patton. The latter did not want Bradley as an emissary from Eisenhower, and had asked that he be appointed as deputy corps commander instead. Patton and Bradley had made an able team in re-forming the US Army in North Africa after the Kasserine defeat and Bradley became the II Corps commander when Patton was assigned to plan the US role in the invasion of Sicily as commander of the Seventh Army. Bradley's corps served under Patton during the Sicilian campaign, and Bradley won the respect of Eisenhower for his calm competence and a better grasp of logistics than Patton. Due in part to Patton's self-destructive behavior, Bradley became the obvious choice to lead the US First Army in Normandy. When the US Army in France expanded in July 1944, Bradley had taken command of 12th Army Group, with Lt. Gen. Courtney Hodges in command of First Army and Lt. Gen. George S. Patton in command of the Third Army. Bradley had a sound working relationship with Eisenhower, based on friendship and mutual respect.

George S. Patton

Gen. George S. Patton was a study in contrast to the other two US commanders. Bradley and Eisenhower were from Midwestern farm families with little military tradition. Patton was from a wealthy Southern family and the descendant of a long line of soldiers who had graduated from the prestigious Virginia Military Institute. His grandfather and namesake had been a distinguished commander in the Confederate Army during the US Civil War. Graduating from West Point six years before Eisenhower or Bradley, Patton had commanded the infant US tank force in combat in France in 1918, where he won the Distinguished Service Cross. He had been a prominent cavalry officer during the interwar years, shunning the staff positions in Washington at which both Eisenhower and Bradley excelled. His tank and cavalry experience had led to his command of the new 2nd Armored Division in 1940, at a time when mechanization of the army was a central concern. He had

Commander of the US Third Army, Lt. Gen. George S. Patton, visits the Lorraine battlefront with the XII Corps commander, Maj. Gen. Manton S. Eddy. (US Army)

Patton discussing the conduct of the campaign with the XII Corps commander, Maj. Gen. Manton S. Eddy. After the XX Corps thrust stalled at Metz, Patton placed the emphasis in Lorraine on Eddy's corps, leading to the Arracourt tank battles. (US Army)

Maj. Gen. Lindsay Silvester (left), commander of the 7th Armd. Div., confers with Maj. Gen. Walton H. Walker (right), commander of the XX Corps, near Chartres in late August 1944. Silvester's division hoped to win a quick bridgehead next to Metz, but lack of supplies and worsening weather stalled the Metz assault in early September. (US Army)

attracted national attention for the exploits of his tank units in pre-war exercises, even gracing the cover of *Life* magazine. Patton had been a natural choice to lead the I Armored Corps in North Africa in 1942, and when it came time to replace the II Corps commander after the Kasserine débâcle, Patton had been selected. His inspirational leadership gave the troops confidence, and Eisenhower had selected him to lead the US Seventh Army in the campaign in Sicily. There, his leadership was mixed: he was, if anything, too impetuous and aggressive, and he did not pay sufficient attention to logistics in a war where logistics were often key. His flamboyant style was very different from Bradley's, and his extravagant behavior got him into serious trouble when, during two visits to field hospitals on Sicily, he slapped soldiers with battle fatigue. In an army of citizen-soldiers this would not do, and it had cast a shadow over Patton's future. Eisenhower still valued his aggressiveness and facility with mobile forces, but his impetuousness and impolitic style both on and off the battlefield and his lack of patience for the mundane but essential chores of modern war had limited his rise to army command. He was widely regarded as the US Army's most aggressive and skilled practitioner of mobile warfare, a reflection of his cavalry background. In spite of his reputation as a tank expert, he was not as familiar with tank technology as with mobile tactics. Gen. Bruce Clarke later remarked, "Patton knew as little about tanks as anybody I ever knew."

Patton's Third Army had two corps committed to the Lorraine fighting at the beginning of September, and a third corps still committed to mopping up German coastal pockets in Brittany. The XII Corps had been commanded since 19 August 1944 by Maj. Gen. Manton S. Eddy, a World War I veteran who had commanded infantry divisions in North Africa, Sicily, and Normandy. The XX Corps was commanded by Maj. Gen. Walton Walker, West Point Class of 1912 and a veteran of World War I.

The commander of XV Corps, Maj. Gen. Wade Haislip (to the right), visits the commander of XII Corps, Maj. Gen. Manton Eddy (to the left) shortly after Haislip's corps was added to Patton's Third Army in mid-September to cover the right flank. (US Army)

OPPOSING ARMIES

THE GERMAN ARMY

T he German Army in Lorraine at the beginning of September 1944 was in a shambles, but was beginning to coalesce around defensive lines along the Moselle River. As the month went on, additional units were brought into the area to stabilize the front and to carry out Hitler's planned counteroffensive. By 1944, the Wehrmacht had become a hollow force. The enormous demands of the Eastern Front and Germany's dwindling manpower reserves had led to formation of large numbers of divisions that were often understrength. The sheer size of the force meant that German divisions were not as well equipped as their American opponents. The average German infantry division depended on horse transport and had no armored vehicles. The average US infantry division was motorized and had attached tank or tank destroyer battalions, making it comparable to German panzer grenadier divisions in capability.

The principal formations of the German Army in Lorraine were infantry divisions of three types: divisions shattered in earlier fighting, new Volksgrenadier divisions that had only recently been raised, or divisions withdrawn more or less intact from southern France. As a result, the infantry formations were of very mixed quality. The 16th Inf. Div., for example, was one of the better units. Earlier in 1944, it had been deployed

The main technical advantage enjoyed by the German units in Lorraine was their Panther tank. The thick frontal armor of the Panther was almost unaffected by the most common US tank gun of the period, the 75mm gun, but it was also virtually impervious to the more powerful 76mm guns found on later production M4 medium tanks, M10, and M18 tank destroyers. This captured Panther was subjected to 76mm gun fire in a trial and none of the rounds fully penetrated. As a result, US armored vehicles had to maneuver to hit the thinner side armor, or use other tactical ploys such as white phosphorous smoke rounds to blind the gun sights. (US Army)

A pair of Panther Ausf. G tanks of Pz. Brig. 111 during operations near Parroy in late September 1944. It was a common practice at this stage of the war to cover the tanks heavily in foliage in an attempt to protect them from aircraft attack. (USNA)

on occupation duty near the Bay of Biscay and had retreated eastward in August, losing the equivalent of two infantry battalions in fighting with French partisans. By early September, it had a strength of about 7,000 men, above average for the units in Lorraine. Many of the other infantry divisions retained the names and numbers of earlier formations, but were in fact nearly entirely new formations, rebuilt from scratch. The Volksgrenadier divisions were a last-minute attempt by Hitler to mobilize every able-bodied man for a final, desperate effort to defend Germany. This was really scraping the bottom of the barrel: they came from schools, Luftwaffe units, naval units, static fortress units, and support formations. Some were better than others. For example, the 462nd Volksgrenadier Division contained a regiment drawn from a school for young lieutenants who had earned battlefield commissions on the Eastern Front. In nearly all cases, however, the infantry divisions were very weak in anti-tank guns and field artillery.

The Wehrmacht had a very different replacement policy from the US Army, and divisions remained in the field at strengths far short of the tables of organization and equipment. As a result, the order of battle for the two opposing sides in the campaign is somewhat deceptive, since so many German units were substantially understrength while all US divisions were near strength. No German division on the Western Front was rated by the high command as Kampfwert I – that is, able to carry out an all-out attack. The best infantry divisions in the west were graded as Kampfwert II – capable of limited offensive operations. By the middle of September, German forces in the Lorraine region amounted to the equivalent of eight divisions in the main line of resistance, with a further six division-equivalents in reserve.

While much is often made of "battle experience" when evaluating the combat potential of units, there is a point at which battle experience becomes battle exhaustion, and enthusiasm for combat is replaced by an overwhelming urge for self-preservation. Many German units in Lorraine had the worst of all possible combinations: inexperienced troops mixed with veterans who only weeks before had experienced the nightmare of the Falaise Gap slaughter or the harrowing experience of the destruction of Army Group Center in the east. If there was any common thread holding together the Wehrmacht in September 1944, it was the protection of German soil from the imminent threat of invasion.

The German forces in Lorraine were particularly weak in artillery. The Nineteenth Army had lost 1,316 of their 1,481 artillery pieces during the retreat from southern France. Although artillery was not as central to tactics as in World War I, it was still the dominant killing arm on the battlefield. Much of the field artillery in infantry divisions was horse-drawn, and there were frequent shortages of ammunition due to transportation bottlenecks resulting from Allied fighter-bomber interdiction of the roads and railroads. The German lack of firepower was a decided disadvantage.

Technological innovation in the Wehrmacht had also stagnated in other fields, such as communication. Infantry regiments deployed a signals platoon at regimental level, with field telephones and four radio sections. These sections could be deployed at company level. Most communications were done with field telephones, especially in defensive fighting, but in mobile operations, the Wehrmacht was at a disadvantage. The standard German man-pack field radio was old and cumbersome, requiring two soldiers to carry it, and it relied on AM transmission that was more subject to static than the FM radios used by the US infantry. Although the Wehrmacht did deploy forward artillery observers, their communication net was not as widespread or robust as in the US Army, so attacking German formations could not count on artillery fire support to the extent of their American opponents.

The panzer and panzer grenadier divisions in Lorraine were a very mixed lot. The 17th SS Panzer Grenadier Division "Goetz von Berlichingen" had been thoroughly smashed by the US Army during Operation Cobra near St. Lo in early August. It was re-formed around two SS panzer grenadier brigades brought in from Denmark and fleshed out with Luftwaffe troops and Volksdeutsche from the Balkans. Like all of the

German field artillery was of high quality, but during the Lorraine campaign it was not available in large numbers, and there were frequent ammunition shortages. This is a Rheinmetall 150mm Kanone 18, the standard Wehrmacht fieldpiece for corps level artillery units. This particular example was captured with several others and used by the US Army's 344th Field Artillery Battalion during the Lorraine fighting until the ammunition ran out. (US Army)

panzer grenadier divisions in this sector, it had little armor: four Pz IV/70 tank destroyers, 12 StuG III assault guns, and 12 FlakPz 38(t) anti-aircraft tanks. The 3rd and 15th Panzer Grenadier Divisions had been stationed in southern France, and had withdrawn in good order into Lorraine. Both divisions were up to strength in troops, and both had a battalion of the new Pz IV/70 tank destroyers. The 15th Pz. Gren. Div. had a battalion of 36 PzKpfw IV tanks, while the 3rd Pz. Gren. Div. had a battalion of StuG III assault guns.

The 11th Panzer Division was widely regarded as the best tank unit in German service in this sector. Like the two panzer grenadier divisions, it had withdrawn from southern France in good order, but in the process had lost much of its tank strength. Starting with about 60-70 tanks, by the time it was committed to the fighting in Lorraine in mid-September, it was down to 50 tanks, of which 30 were Panthers. The 21st Panzer Division had been heavily committed to the fighting in Normandy and after suffering stiff losses had not been brought back up to strength. It had no tanks at the beginning of the month, though its StugAbt 200 (assault gun battalion) had several StuG III assault guns by mid-month.

As of 20 August 1944, there were only 184 tanks and assault guns on the entire Western Front. This would change by the middle of September as more armor was rushed forward. The plan was to increase the strength in the west to 712 tanks and assault guns by early September in order to carry out Hitler's directives for a Lorraine counteroffensive. Tank production in Germany reached record levels in 1944, thanks to the belated industrial rationalization of Albert Speer. At the same time, however, fuel and manpower shortages meant that there were not enough trained crews or trained tank unit officers to replace the heavy losses in experienced troops. The quality of German tank crews fell steadily in 1944, especially after the summer 1944 disasters. The problem was not the lack of tanks but the lack of tank crews.

The bulk of the German tank strength in Lorraine was located in the new panzer brigades. They had been organized earlier in the summer on Hitler's personal instructions and against the advice of the inspector of the panzer forces, Gen. Heinz Guderian. These brigades were given priority in assignments from the summer's tank production instead of replacing losses in the regular panzer divisions. Most were formed around the remnants of units that had been destroyed in the débâcle on the Eastern Front in June and July, when Army Group Center had been destroyed.

The first batch of these brigades, numbered from 101 to 110, were in fact closer to a regiment in strength, with only a single tank battalion. Equipment included 36 Panthers, 11 Pz IV/70 tank destroyers and four Flakpanzers for air defense. The later brigades, numbered above 110, had two tank battalions: one of PzKpfw IV and one of PzKpfw V Panthers. Three of the four brigades used in the Lorraine fighting were of this heavier configuration. On paper at least, these were formidable formations, with 90 tanks and 10 tank destroyers—much more armor than most German panzer divisions of the time possessed. But they were slapdash formations suffering from poor organization and inadequate training. The panzer brigades were intended to be used on the Eastern Front as a potent mobile reserve which could staunch gaps in the line. As a result, they were not well-balanced combined arms forces like normal panzer divisions, but were heavy in tanks and weak in infantry, artillery, reconnaissance, and support. The brigade staff was completely inadequate and the brigade commanders had a difficult time communicating and directing their units. As was the tendency on the Eastern Front, anti-tank weapons had been given more attention than field artillery, and the brigade lacked field artillery fire-support. In addition there was little in the way of reconnaissance units in the brigades; this would become evident in the Lorraine fighting. The brigades also suffered from a lack of tank recovery vehicles and maintenance equipment, which exacerbated their losses in combat, since damaged vehicles could not easily be recovered and were often abandoned.

The brigades were raised in various locations across Germany, and the brigade commanders seldom met their subordinate commanders or their component units until they disembarked from trains in the staging areas leading into Lorraine. Manteuffel later wrote that the panzer brigades would have been effective units on the Eastern Front, an interesting comment considering his extensive experience in that theater. In the west, against a very different opponent, they would prove to be a major disappointment.

Part of the problem of the German forces in the Lorraine counter-offensive was the "Eastern" outlook of many of the units. Manteuffel himself had been brought in from Poland only days before the start of the attack, and the new brigade commanders and many of their troops were veterans of the Eastern Front. While quite prepared to deal with the Red Army, they were unfamiliar with the US Army and its very different tactics and fighting abilities. This would quickly become evident in their use of armor. On the Eastern Front, it was not unusual to use tank formations as a shock force to punch through the emaciated Red Army infantry formations. The Red Army was poorly provided with modern anti-tank weapons and had very limited capability to call in either artillery support or close-air support. This was not the case with the US Army, as would become apparent over the following month.

The Luftwaffe would not prove to be of any use in the ensuing battles. The fighter and fighter-bomber force in France was under the control of Jagdkorps II, while fighters in neighboring Germany deployed for defense of the Reich were controlled by Jagdkorps I. On 29 August 1944, the advance of Allied forces had obliged Jagdkorps II to order all remaining fighter-bomber units out of France and into western Germany. At the beginning of September, there were about 420 fighters and fighter-bombers in this force, of which about 110 covered the Nancy-Metz area of Lorraine.

Unlike the US Army, the Wehrmacht received very little air support during the Lorraine fighting. As with the tanks, this was not so much from lack of aircraft production as from a shortage of trained pilots. The Luftwaffe had suffered massive losses in air battles over the Reich since the spring of 1944, and this had been further accelerated by the summer fighting. To make matters worse, a fuel crisis in August further curtailed training. German aircraft production reached record levels in the summer of 1944, but this did not translate into a readily useful force. US aircraft encountered the Luftwaffe in large numbers on only two occasions during the Lorraine fighting in September, and found that the pilots were inexperienced and vulnerable. Besides the sheer lack of experienced pilots, the Luftwaffe's fighter-bomber force had atrophied badly by 1944, due in part to the heavy concentration on fighter aviation for defense of the Reich. There was no standardized means for ground direction of close-air support, and despite frequent army calls for air support, none was forthcoming except for a few rare occasions when key bridges were attacked.

The geography of Lorraine held mixed opportunities for both sides. From the German perspective, the Moselle valley formed a natural defense line, since the river has a high rate of flow, many potential crossing sites are wooded, the river banks have a high gradient, and most crossing sites are covered by hills on the east bank. It was particularly formidable in the northern portion of the sector, and likely river crossings were covered by the artillery in the Metz fortresses. Germany had controlled the area around Metz from 1870 to 1918 and again after 1940, so the most modern defenses faced west. The Metz-Thionville Stellung was the major defensive obstacle in Lorraine. The traditional capital of Lorraine, Nancy, has not been fortified in modern times, but the river lines and the plateau of the Massif de Haye on its west bank serve as a significant natural obstacle. The ground most suitable for mobile operations was in the southern sector between Toul and Epinal. This region, known to French planners as the Trouée de Charmes, or the Charmes Gap, had been a traditional battlefield, most recently, three decades before when the German Army had been defeated there in the opening phases of World War I. The area held by Nineteenth Army was notionally located within the defenses of the so-called Kitzinger Line, which had been constructed starting in early August. In reality, there were no substantial new defenses. The weather slightly favored the Germans: September 1944 was unusually wet and foggy, which would severely limit Allied close-air support.

THE US ARMY

Patton's Third Army entered the Lorraine campaign with two corps; its third corps was laying siege to German garrisons at Brest, on the coast. In September 1944, the US Army was in excellent shape after a triumphant dash across France the previous month. The divisions in Patton's Third Army were generally in better condition than those in Hodges' First Army, which had experienced the brutal close-country bocage fighting in June and July 1944. In marked contrast to the German units, which were seldom at full organizational strength, the US Third Army had not yet encountered the personnel shortages that would afflict them in the late autumn. Unit cohesion, training, and morale were generally excellent.

German and American infantry tactics differed in significant ways. The German infantry squad was trained to use their MG 42s as the centerpiece of their tactics, based on World War I experiences which emphasized the importance of machine-guns in infantry combat. In a platoon action, one of the squads would often be equipped with the headquarters' machine-gun, allowing it to serve as the focal point. US tactical doctrine placed emphasis on the individual rifleman, armed with the semi-automatic M1 Garand rifle, rather than the BAR squad automatic rifle. Although the US M1 Garand had a higher rate of fire than the bolt-action German 98k rifle,

The workhorse of the US divisional artillery batteries was the M2A1 105mm howitzer. This weapon could fire a 33lb high-explosive round to a range of about 12,000 yards. Each infantry division had 54 of these plus 12 of the heavier 155mm howitzers. Of these, 36 105mm howitzers were found in the divisional artillery, while six 105mm howitzers were deployed in a cannon company in each infantry regiment. (US Army)

US infantry squads were seldom able to achieve firepower superiority over their German opponents due to the lethality of the German machine-gun tactics.

Nevertheless, US infantry formations often enjoyed significant firepower advantages over their German opponents. What the squad and platoon lacked in organic firepower was made up in artillery support. While German and American artillery divisions had similar artillery strength on paper, in reality the US divisions were more likely to actually have their establishment of weapons – and more often had adequate ammunition supplies. However, the real advantage in infantry combat was communications, especially in mobile operations. The US infantry had far better and more lavish radio equipment than the Germans. At platoon level, the US Army used the SCR-536 "handie-talkie", a small hand-held AM transceiver. At company level, they used the man-pack SCR-300 "walkie-talkie" FM transceiver to communicate with the battalion and higher headquarters. The German Army had no platoon radios, and their older AM man-pack radios were deployed no lower than at company level. The widespread use of dependable radios meant that US infantry could call for fire support during mobile offensive operations much more easily than their German counterparts.

In another important tactical innovation, the US Army in Europe regularly deployed an artillery forward observer team with forward infantry companies. The officer was equipped with a man-portable radio linked to the artillery net, and was assigned both to call in and to correct fire. American units in key sectors also enjoyed the added firepower of corps artillery, and infantry divisions often had additional artillery battalions allotted to their support for special missions. US infantry also

had better armored support, often having a tank battalion and tank destroyer battalion added to each division.

The German infantry tended to hold a disparaging view of American infantry, judging them to be less aggressive in close-combat tactics. This was in part a reflection of the stagnation in German infantry tactics. Experienced US infantry units, painfully aware of their firepower shortcomings when up against German infantry squads, were perfectly happy to use the killing power of artillery when it was available instead of suffering needless casualties. This difference in outlook was in part a cultural clash: the pragmatism of the GI versus the romantic fighting spirit of the German *Landser* (fighting man).

The US armored divisions were far better equipped than their German counterparts in September 1944, being close to establishment strength, and they fought differently. US doctrine held that the penetration of the enemy main line of resistance would be carried out by infantry backed by separate tank battalions and artillery. US armored divisions were held in reserve for exploitation after the penetration had been achieved. German panzer divisions were frequently used to win the penetration, a tactic that had proven increasingly costly as the war went on and infantry anti-tank tactics and technology improved. As a result, US armored divisions were not generally employed like the panzer brigades in Lorraine as a shock force to overcome enemy infantry formations. In this respect, the US was closer to the Red Army's tank corps in doctrine than to the German practices. US armored divisions were true combined-arms teams, especially when compared to the tank-poor German panzer divisions and tank-heavy panzer brigades. It is often forgotten that each US armored division had the same number of artillery and armored infantry battalions as tank battalions – three each. In addition, US armored divisions were often reinforced with additional infantry or artillery for specific missions.

The US Army enjoyed advantages in communications, with more advanced equipment like the SCR-300 "walkie-talkie" radio. This was the first widely used FM infantry radio, and offered better performance than the German AM radios. It is seen here in use near Vagney, France, on 17 October 1944. (US Army)

The US Army had a significant advantage over the Wehrmacht in artillery, both in terms of quantity and quality. US heavy artillery was mechanized, using fully tracked tractors like this M4 high speed tractor towing an 8-in. howitzer of the 999th Field Artillery Battalion (Colored) near Nantes-Gassicourt on 20 August 1944. (US Army)

The primary US combat unit was the combat command. Each combat command was tailored to the tactical mission but generally included a tank battalion, an armored infantry battalion, and an armored field artillery battalion. Other units could be added from division or corps. For example, during part of the Lorraine fighting, the 4th Armored Division's Combat Command A had three artillery battalions at its disposal. Each division normally employed three combat commands, CCA, CCB, and CCR. In some divisions, all three combat commands were in combat at one time. The 4th Armd. Div., which bore the brunt of the Lorraine tank fighting, used its structure in the intended fashion, with the CCR serving as a reserve. Battle-weary battalions would periodically be cycled through the CCR to prevent the corrosive effects of battle exhaustion.

In terms of weaponry, the German panzer force enjoyed a significant technological advantage with its Panther tank. US tank design had stagnated during the war years because of the failure of the Army Ground Forces and the armored force to absorb and learn from the advances in tank technology. As a result, the armored divisions in Lorraine were using essentially the same M4 medium tank as had been standard in Tunisia two years before. New M4 medium tanks were becoming available with the newer 76mm gun, but they were not numerous, their armor was not improved, and their armor penetration capability was inferior to the German Panther's long 75mm gun. The M4 with 76mm gun was disparaged by Patton, and was not initially popular in the 4th Armored Division. Tankers felt that the 75mm gun was more versatile than the 76mm gun, which was optimized for tank fighting only. In a head-to-head tank fight at normal combat ranges, the Panther was impervious to the M4 tank's 75mm gun, but the Panther could destroy the M4 tank frontally at any reasonable combat range. The main advantage enjoyed by US tankers compared to German panzer crews in 1944 was superior training. German fuel supplies were so low and training time so short that the quality of German tank crews had declined precipitously since the glory days of 1939-42. German tanks were still very dangerous because of their technological advantage, or when used from defilade, but in Lorraine, the US tankers usually prevailed. Innovative tactics played an important part. A popular tactic in experienced US tank battalions when encountering Panthers was to strike them first with white phosphorous smoke rounds. Inexperienced German crews would sometimes be forced out by the acrid smoke, drawn in through the tank's ventilator. Even if these tricks did not work, the smoke prevented the Panthers from locating their opponents, giving the M4 tanks time to maneuver to the flanks or rear, where their 75mm gun could penetrate the Panther's armor. This tactic was standard operating procedure in some units, including CCA, 4th Armored Division. Some US tank units preferred to fire high-explosive rounds at the Panther, finding that inexperienced German crews would simply abandon their tank.

US tankers enjoyed the same communications advantage as the US infantry. Their tanks used modern FM radios, and better radio communications meant that tank companies could call for artillery fire support, and in some cases close-air support, to carry out their mission. This was often the case when a column was stopped by hidden German armor in defilade position, which could not be easily eliminated by direct tank fire. Each tank battalion had a platoon of M4 tanks with

105mm howitzers in the headquarters company, and most combat commands had at least one battalion of self-propelled M7 105mm howitzer motor carriages for each tank battalion, sometimes more. US armored divisions had advantages in less recognized areas as well. Armored units were better supplied with engineer equipment, which was essential in mobile operations for river crossing. An important innovation was the engineer's treadway bridge, which could be broken down into loads small enough to fit into standard $2\frac{1}{2}$-ton trucks. Coincidentally, it was the commander of Patton's spearhead formation, Col. Bruce Clarke, an engineer by training, who had been the army's prime advocate for the development of rapid bridging equipment for the armored force.

The US Army had the greater number of tanks in the Lorraine sector. German strength was never more than 350 tanks, even at the peak of the tank fighting in the third week of September. The Third Army started out the campaign with about 165 M5A1 light tanks, 596 M4 (75mm) and 76 M4 (76mm) medium tanks, and about 450 M10 and M18 tank destroyers. About 40 percent of the tanks were in separate tank battalions supporting the infantry, and the remainder were in the armored divisions.

If there was one combat arm in which the US Army had unquestioned superiority over the Wehrmacht, it was the artillery. This was not simply a question of quantity. The US field artillery battalions were more modern than their German counterparts in nearly all respects. While their cannon were not significantly different in capability, the US field artillery battalions were entirely motorized, while German field artillery, especially infantry division units, was still horse-drawn. US heavy artillery was mechanized, using fully tracked high-speed tractors. The high level of motorization provided mobility for the batteries, and also ensured supply.

The US field artillery also enjoyed a broader and more modern assortment of communication equipment. Another US innovation was the fire direction center (FDC). Located at battalion, division, and corps level, the FDC concentrated the analog computers and other calculation devices alongside the communication equipment, permitting prompt receipt of messages and prompt calculation of fire missions. This level of communication allowed new tactics, the most lethal of which was TOT or "time-on-target." Field artillery is most effective when the first few rounds catch the enemy out in the open. Once the first few rounds have landed, enemy troops take cover, and the rate of casualties to subsequent fire declines dramatically. The aim of TOT was to deliver the fire on the target simultaneously, even from separate batteries. TOT fire missions were more lethal and more economical of ammunition than traditional staggered fire-strikes, and effective communication meant that the batteries could switch targets rapidly as well.

Another firepower advantage enjoyed by the US Army in the Lorraine fighting was air support. The US Army Air Forces tactical air commands (TAC) were structured to operate in direct support of a single army. As a result, Patton's Third Army had Brig. Gen. Otto Weyland's XIX TAC attached. US tactical air units were more tightly integrated than in any other army, and Weyland's command was co-located with Patton's headquarters. The XIX TAC generally had about 400 aircraft available, usually organized into two fighter wings, each organized into groups with an average of three fighter squadrons per group. A fighter squadron had 25 aircraft; a squadron mission typically employed 12 fighters; and a group mission used 36. At the beginning of September, XIX TAC had seven fighter groups and one photo reconnaissance group. The majority of the XIX TAC squadrons were equipped with the P-47 Thunderbolt fighter-bomber to provide close support and interdiction using heavy machine-gun fire, bombs, napalm, and rockets. There were also one or two squadrons of P-51s, which were used to provide tactical air cover as well as "fast reconnaissance," including spotting for the corps' heavy 240mm guns. The XIX TAC conducted a larger proportion of close-air support missions out of their total combat missions than any other TAC in Europe.

The XIX TAC deployed 20 radio teams with the ground units: one team per corps and infantry division headquarters, two with each armored division (with each combat command), and one with each cavalry group when they were performing key screening or holding missions. The team was based around a radio crew that linked the division to the XIX TAC headquarters by means of a SCR-624 radio installed in the division's truck-mounted SCR-399 "doghouse." The tactical air liaison officers (TALO) operated from "veeps" – jeeps with a rack-mounted SCR-522 VHF aircraft radio. They deployed forward with advancing units so that they could vector attacking fighter-bombers onto targets much in the same fashion as artillery forward observers.

The effectiveness of close-air support in World War II remains controversial. Both the Allies and the Germans tended to exaggerate its power: the US air force in its post-war struggle to become a separate service, the Germans as an excuse for poor battlefield performance. Wartime and post-war operational studies have concluded that the ability of fighter-bombers to knock out tanks on the battlefield was greatly exaggerated. In a post-battle survey after the Ardennes fighting in 1945 of a XIX TAC sector, it was found that aircraft had knocked out about six armored vehicles of the 90 claimed. The munitions of the day – unguided rockets, bombs, and heavy machine-guns – were not sufficiently accurate or sufficiently powerful to destroy many tanks. On the other hand, fighter-bombers had an enormous psychological impact, bolstering the morale of GIs and terrifying the average German soldier. German field commanders spoke of the fear instilled by close-air attack in much the same way as they spoke of the "tank panic" of the 1939-41 blitzkrieg years, and as in the case of tank panic, the psychological effects of close-air attack lessened quickly through experience.

The most effective employment of close-air support was to attack supply columns, storage areas, and other soft targets. Even if not particularly effective against the tanks themselves, fighter-bombers could severely limit the mobility of panzer units by forcing them to conduct road marches only at night. Furthermore, the avaricious demand for fuel and ammunition in modern armies made them very vulnerable to supply cut-offs. A panzer brigade could be rendered as ineffective by destroying its trucks and supply vehicles as by destroying the tanks themselves. The commander of CCA of the 4th Armd. Div., Col. Bruce Clarke, later remarked, "We were certainly glad to have [close-air support] but I would say their effect was certainly not decisive in any place."

Besides the fighter-bombers, US divisions had organic aviation in the form of L-4 (Piper Cub) and other liaison aircraft, popularly called "Flying Grasshoppers." These were primarily used to correct field artillery and conduct artillery reconnaissance. Col. Clarke flew ahead of his advancing tank columns in one, enabling him to direct the columns with precision.

GERMAN ORDER OF BATTLE, 16 SEPTEMBER 1944*

Army Group G: Generaloberst Johannes Blaskowitz

First Army: General der Panzertruppe Otto von Knobelsdorff

80th Corps	**General der Infanterie Dr. Franz Bayer**
5th Fallschirmjaeger Division	Generalmajor Ludwig Heilmann
Panzer Lehr Division (battlegroup)	
82nd Corps	**General der Artillerie Johann Sinnhuber**
19th Volksgrenadier Division	Generalleutnant Karl Wissmath
36th Volksgrenadier Division	Generalmajor August Welln
559th Volksgrenadier Division	Generalmajor Baron Kurt von Muhlen
13th SS Corps	**Generalleutnant der Waffen-SS Herman Priess**
3rd Panzer Grenadier Division	Generalmajor Hans Hecker
15th Panzer Grenadier Division	Generalleutnant Eberhard Rodt
17th SS Panzer Grenadier Division	
"Goetz von Berlichingen"	Oberst Eduard Deisenhofer
462nd Volksgrenadier Division	Generalleutnant Vollrath Lubbe
553rd Volksgrenadier Division	Oberst Enrich von Loesch
106th Panzer Brigade	
"Feldherrnhalle"	Oberst Franz Bake

Fifth Panzer Army: General der Panzertruppe Hasso von Manteuffel

47th Panzer Corps: General der Panzertruppen Heinrich Freiherr von Luettwitz

21st Panzer Division	Generalleutnant Edgar Feuchtinger
111th Panzer Brigade	Oberst Heinrich von Bronsart-Schellendorf
112th Panzer Brigade	Oberst Horst von Usedom
113th Panzer Brigade	Oberst Erich von Seckendorff

Nineteenth Army: General der Infanterie Friederich Weise

66th Corps **General der Artillerie Walter Lucht**
16th Infantry Division General der Infanterie Ernst Haechel
Kampfgruppe Ottenbacher Generalleutnant Ernst Ottenbacher
Elements of 15th Panzer Grenadiers, 21st Panzer

64th Corps **General der Pionere Karl Sachs**
716th Infantry Division Generalleutnant Wilhelm Richter
189th Reserve Division Generalmajor Bogislav von Schwerin

85th Corps **Generalleutnant Baptist Kneiss**
11th Panzer Division Generalleutnant Wend von Wietersheim

4th Luftwaffe Field Corps **Generalleutnant Erich Petersen**
338th Infantry Division Generalleutnant Flottmann
159th Reserve Division Generalleutnant Albin Nake
198th Infantry Division Generalmajor Otto Richter

* German Order of Battle only lists those units opposite the US Army's Third Army in Lorraine

US ARMY ORDER OF BATTLE*
12th Army Group: General Omar Bradley

Third Army: Lt. Gen. George S. Patton

XX Corps Maj. Gen. Walton Walker
2nd Cavalry Reconnaissance Group Col. W. P. Withers
7th Armored Division Maj. Gen. Lindsay Silvester
5th Infantry Division Maj. Gen. Stafford Irwin
90th Infantry Division Maj. Gen. Raymond McClain

XII Corps Maj. Gen. Manton S. Eddy
106th Cavalry Reconnaissance Group Col. Vennard Wilson
4th Armored Division Maj. Gen. John Wood
6th Armored Division Maj. Gen. Robert Grow
35th Infantry Division Maj. Gen. Paul Baade
80th Infantry Division Maj. Gen. Horace McBride

XV Corps Maj. Gen. Wade Haislip
79th Infantry Division Maj. Gen. Ira Wyche
French 2nd Armored Division Maj. Gen. Jacques Leclerc

XIX Tactical Air Command Brig. Gen. Otto P. Weyland
100th Fighter Wing
303rd Fighter Wing

*US Army Order of Battle only lists those units in the US Army's Third Army in Lorraine

OPENING MOVES

Approaching the Moselle

At the beginning of September 1944, Patton's Third Army had halted after having crossed the Meuse River. Priority for supply in Bradley's 12th Army Group went to Hodges' neighboring First Army, to support its drive towards Aachen, which covered the right flank of Montgomery's 21st Army Group. By 4 September, Montgomery's forces were well over the Seine and German reserves in Belgium had been enveloped by Collins' VII Corps near Mons. Eisenhower decided that under such favorable circumstances the original SHAEF conception of a two-axis thrust towards Germany could be supported, so Third Army would receive equal support priority to Hodges' First Army. While this did not end the supply crisis, it allowed the Third Army to resume offensive operations on a limited scale.

"Reconnaissance-in-force" operations were planned to see if bridgeheads could be secured over the Moselle before the Germans could erect sufficient defenses. The objectives of Walker's XX Corps

The terrain in Lorraine consisted of rolling farmland, with many hills. Here, officers of the 80th Inf. Div. have set up an observation post on a hill overlooking the countryside around Montsec on 3 September 1944. (US Army)

Reconnaissance was a vital requirement in the Lorraine fighting, and the hard-pressed cavalry squadrons seldom enjoyed the recognition they deserved for their dangerous and demanding assignment. They were equipped with M8 light armored cars, like the one seen here, and machine-gun armed jeeps. Here, the crew of an M8 armored car of the 80th Division's reconnaissance troop enjoy some snacks from an American Red Cross worker near the Moselle River on 8 September 1944. (US Army)

opposite the fortified city of Metz proved the most difficult. Walker hoped that a Moselle bridgehead could be secured with a rapid armor thrust, as had already worked on the Marne and the Meuse in August, but probes by cavalry squadrons on 5 September made clear that the Germans would not easily be pushed aside. Attacks by the 7th Armd. Div.'s CCB finally reached the banks of the Moselle south of Fort Driant in the early hours of 7 September, followed by CCA's drive to the river north of Arnaville. On the corps' left flank, north of Metz, the 90th Inf. Div. began moving from Etain towards Thionville on the Moselle River.

Although the German forces had been holding the Moselle River line successfully for most of the day, the new German First Army commander, Gen. Knobelsdorff, wanted more vigorous action. He contacted the Führer headquarters with a plan to stage a spoiling attack by turning the flank of Walker's XX Corps with a tank attack from the west bank of the Moselle. He intended to use Pz. Brig. 106, which had been reserved for use in the forthcoming Lorraine counteroffensive, so the effort required Hitler's direct approval. This was granted late on 7 September, with the proviso that the brigade could be used for only 48 hours before being returned to the reserve.

Pz. Brig. 106 had been formed around remnants of the Panzer Grenadier Division Feldherrnhalle that had been encircled and destroyed in July 1944 in Byelorussia during Operation Bagration. It was commanded by one of the most distinguished Wehrmacht tank commanders, Col. Dr Franz Bake. He had won the Iron Cross First and Second Class as an infantryman in World War I, and had commanded a PzKpfw 35(t) company in France in 1940. He had also led a panzer battalion in the climactic tank encounter at Prokhorovka during the 1943 Kursk battles, and then the legendary Heavy Panzer Regiment Bake on the Eastern Front in 1944. He had been decorated with the Knight's Cross in January 1943 and the Oak Leaves in August 1943, and was only

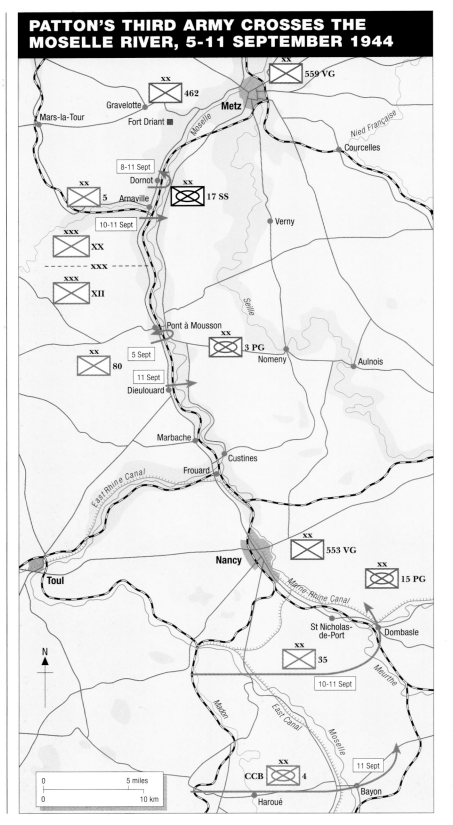

PATTON'S THIRD ARMY CROSSES THE MOSELLE RIVER, 5-11 SEPTEMBER 1944

Mars-la-Tour

Gravelotte

462

Metz

XX 559 VG

Fort Driant

Moselle

Courcelles

Nied Française

8-11 Sept

Dornot

XX 5

Arnaville

XX 17 SS

Verny

10-11 Sept

XXX XX

XXX

XXX XII

Seille

Pont à Mousson

XX 3 PG

Nomeny

Aulnois

5 Sept

XX 80

11 Sept

Dieulouard

Marbache

Custines

East Rhine Canal

Frouard

Nancy

XX 553 VG

Toul

Marne-Rhine Canal

XX 15 PG

St Nicholas-de-Port

Dombasle

XX 35

Meurthe

10-11 Sept

Madon

East Canal

Moselle

N

CCB XX 4

11 Sept

Bayon

0 ___ 5 miles

0 ___ 10 km

Haroué

ABOVE **An M1 57mm anti-tank gun covers an intersection in Algrange during the fighting between the 358th Infantry of the 90th Division and the 559th Volksgrenadier Division on 10-12 September. The 57mm gun was a license copy of the British 6-pdr anti-tank gun and was the standard anti-tank weapon of infantry divisions in 1944. There were 18 in each regiment, three per battalion. The 90th Division also had an attached towed**

3-in. tank destroyer battalion to supplement their firepower. (US Army)

BELOW **The town of Mairy is surrounded by hills on all sides. This is a view looking north into the town from route D145 from Mainville, as would have been seen by the panzer grenadiers entering the town from this direction during the 8 September attack. (S. Zaloga)**

the 49th German soldier of the war to receive the Swords to the Knight's Cross, in February 1944. He had been assigned command of Pz. Brig. 106 when it was raised near Danzig in July 1944. The brigade had received its Panther tanks in early August, but lack of fuel had meant that there had been little tactical training. The brigade had one of the most experienced cadres of any of the new units, with other Knight's Cross holders – Erich Oberwohrmann commanding the Panther regiment and Ewald Bartel serving as the brigade adjutant.

The target of the panzer attack was the 90th Inf. Div., who called themselves the "Tough Ombres" after their divisional insignia – a superimposed "T" and "O" symbolizing their recruitment area in Texas and Oklahoma. The division had a bad reputation due to its poor combat performance in Normandy. Within six weeks of landing, it had lost the equivalent of 100 percent of its strength and some rifle companies had suffered casualties the equivalent of 400 percent of their establishment strength. The original divisional commander had been sacked and his replacement was a National Guardsman, a banker from Oklahoma, Brig. Gen. Raymond McLain. It was unusual for National Guard officers to receive divisional command, and the appointment was a testament to McLain's earlier achievements in the Mediterranean theater. Under new leadership, the division's performance improved markedly during the fighting for the Falaise Gap, and by September, it was a well-led, combat-hardened unit. The 90th Inf. Div. was the northernmost division of XX Corps, positioned on its exposed left flank as it moved towards Thionville.

Pz. Brig. 106 was equipped with 36 Panthers, 11 Pz IV/70 (V) tank destroyers, and 119 armored half-tracks. The attack was ordered for the night of 6 September, but was delayed by the late arrival of the 59th Infantry Regiment. There was no space in the half-tracks for these troops, so they rode into action on the Panther tanks. After a foray on

A GI from the 90th Inf. Div. inspects some of the German equipment captured by the division during the fighting with Pz. Brig. 106 near Mairy. These are both armed versions of the standard German Hanomag SdKfz 251 Ausf. D armored infantry half-track. An SdKfz 251/21 anti-aircraft vehicle with a triple MG151 30mm cannon mounting is seen to the left. Pz. Gren. Bn. 2106 had ten of the SdKfz 251/9 Stummel assault gun armed with a close support 75mm howitzer, seen on the right. (US Army)

the afternoon of 7 September, in which they failed to locate US forces, they were ordered to stage a second attack later in the evening in support of the 19th Volksgrenadier Division. Due to the fluid nature of the lines, the unit began its attack from the north of the advancing American forces, against their exposed flank. Late on the night of 7/8 September, Pz. Brig. 106 began its move southward from Audun-le-Roman towards Briey in two columns, the Stossgruppe 1 (attack group 1) advancing via Mont-Bonvilliers, and the Stossgruppe 2 via Trieux. The attack was preceded by little or no reconnaissance, and at about 0200 the main column split in two near Murville, part of the force moving down the main route N43 and the other moving along a small country road towards the villages of Mont and Mairy.

The headquarters of the 90th Inf. Div. was bivouacked on a wooded hill south-east of Landres, flanked by roads on either side. Columns from Stossgruppe 1 of Pz. Brig. 106 began moving down these same roads around 0200. The area is hilly and wooded, and the German armored column moved past the scattered headquarter units without either side noticing until 0300. The crewman on a M4 medium tank guarding the divisional artillery HQ realized that the column was German and fired at the trailing vehicle. The German half-track exploded in flames, but the fire illuminated the American tank, which was then brought under fire from the lead Panther tanks. The US tank exploded, and casualties among the artillery staff were heavy. Stossgruppe 1 continued to move south-eastward towards Briey, but much more cautiously. The divisional headquarters personnel, supported by some tanks from the 712th Tank Bn., began attacking the tail-end of the German formation while at the same time warning the neighboring infantry battalions. The nearby 712th Tank Bn. was dispersed, but the tankers were reluctant to fire in the dark for fear of fratricide.

In the pre-dawn darkness, the Panther tanks and panzer grenadiers became spread out across the countryside as the Americans rallied. Instead of retreating in the face of a surprise night-attack, as the

ABOVE **The attack on Mairy was broken up with support from the 607th Tank Destroyer Battalion. This unit was equipped with the M6 3-in. anti-tank gun, as seen here during training exercises with the 614th Tank Destroyer Battalion (Colored) on 23 September. (US Army)**

RIGHT **The 90th Inf. Div. was the northernmost of Patton's divisions during the attempts to cross the Moselle, and was the subject of the first panzer attack near Mairy on the night of 7/8 September. After crushing this attack, the division continued to move towards Thionville. These troops are from the division's 358th Infantry Regiment and are taking shelter in a trench leading into an old German bunker with the inscription *Viel feind, viel Her* ('Many enemies, much honor'). (US Army)**

Germans had expected, the American infantry began methodically to attack the intruder. After daybreak, the left wing of Stossgruppe 1 began an attack on the village of Mairy, occupied by the 1st Battalion, 358th Infantry, which was supported by a platoon of towed 3-in. anti-tank guns from the 607th Tank Destroyer Battalion. Mairy is in a depression surrounded by hills. The Panther spearhead began firing at the village from the high ground near Mont around 0700, but they were brought under fire from the anti-tank guns and two German tanks were knocked

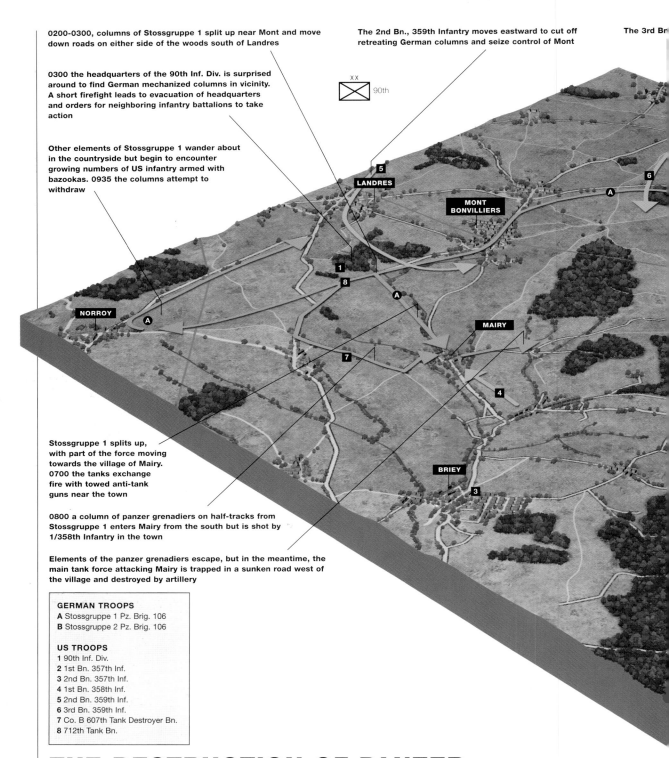

0200-0300, columns of Stossgruppe 1 split up near Mont and move down roads on either side of the woods south of Landres

The 2nd Bn., 359th Infantry moves eastward to cut off retreating German columns and seize control of Mont

The 3rd Br

0300 the headquarters of the 90th Inf. Div. is surprised around to find German mechanized columns in vicinity. A short firefight leads to evacuation of headquarters and orders for neighboring infantry battalions to take action

Other elements of Stossgruppe 1 wander about in the countryside but begin to encounter growing numbers of US infantry armed with bazookas. 0935 the columns attempt to withdraw

Stossgruppe 1 splits up, with part of the force moving towards the village of Mairy. 0700 the tanks exchange fire with towed anti-tank guns near the town

0800 a column of panzer grenadiers on half-tracks from Stossgruppe 1 enters Mairy from the south but is shot by 1/358th Infantry in the town

Elements of the panzer grenadiers escape, but in the meantime, the main tank force attacking Mairy is trapped in a sunken road west of the village and destroyed by artillery

GERMAN TROOPS
A Stossgruppe 1 Pz. Brig. 106
B Stossgruppe 2 Pz. Brig. 106

US TROOPS
1 90th Inf. Div.
2 1st Bn. 357th Inf.
3 2nd Bn. 357th Inf.
4 1st Bn. 358th Inf.
5 2nd Bn. 359th Inf.
6 3rd Bn. 359th Inf.
7 Co. B 607th Tank Destroyer Bn.
8 712th Tank Bn.

THE DESTRUCTION OF PANZER BRIGADE 106, 8 SEPTEMBER 1944

In an attempt tp prevent Walker's XX Corps reaching the Moselle River, Gen. Knobelsdorff used Pz. Brig. 106 to launch a spoiling attack. This was driven back by the US 90th Inf. Div.

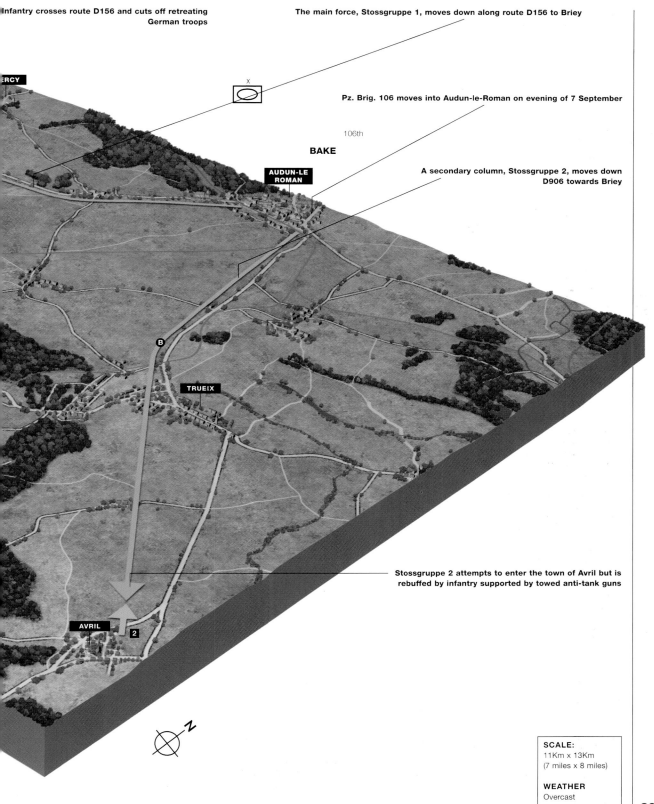

Infantry crosses route D156 and cuts off retreating German troops

The main force, Stossgruppe 1, moves down along route D156 to Briey

Pz. Brig. 106 moves into Audun-le-Roman on evening of 7 September

106th

BAKE

A secondary column, Stossgruppe 2, moves down D906 towards Briey

ERCY

AUDUN-LE ROMAN

B

TRUEIX

Stossgruppe 2 attempts to enter the town of Avril but is rebuffed by infantry supported by towed anti-tank guns

AVRIL

2

SCALE:
11Km x 13Km
(7 miles x 8 miles)

WEATHER
Overcast

39

OPPOSITE, TOP **This Panther Ausf. G tank from Pz. Brig. 106 was left abandoned west of Metz after the Mairy fighting. It was left by the roadside with a small sign to serve for vehicle recognition by passing troops. This team from the 5th Division is preparing to remove it in October 1944. (US Army)**

OPPOSITE, BELOW **On 10 September a patrol from the French 2nd Armored Division, the southernmost unit of Patton's Third Army, linked up with a patrol from the 6th Army Group, marking the link-up of the Allied forces from the North Sea to the Mediterranean. Here, a French crew from an M20 armored utility car shake hands with an American crew from an M8 armored car of the US Seventh Army in the streets of Autun. (US Army)**

BELOW **US troops inspect a knocked-out column of armor from the 4th Armd. Div. west of Nancy, France, on 10 September during the initial stages of the Moselle River operations. The M3A1 half-track has been hit by a high explosive round which has caved in the side armor and set the vehicle on fire. (US Army)**

out. A panzer grenadier company attempted to outflank the anti-tank defenses, barreling into the town from the south along the Mainville road on 11 SdKfz 251 armored half-tracks around 0800. Two were blown apart at close range by the US infantry supported by the 105mm howitzers of their cannon company, two more were knocked out by bazooka fire from the tank destroyer platoon, and four more were lost to 3-in. anti-tank guns as they tried to retreat out of the town to the north. A portion of the main column led by Panther tanks attempted to infiltrate towards the village down a sunken farm road around 0850. The lead Panther was disabled by an infantry team, and before the column could extract itself from the gully, a forward observer from the 949th Field Artillery directed fire on it. Over 300 rounds of 155mm howitzer fire pummeled the column, knocking out five Panthers and 20 half-tracks. The fighting around Mairy cost Pz. Brig. 106 seven Panther tanks and 48 half-tracks.

While this fight was taking place, the 2nd Battalion, 359th Infantry was sealing off escape routes behind the German advance. With the left column shattered in its ill-fated attack on Mairy, the scattered right wing was being trapped. The 90th Division HQ was reinforced with tanks from the 712th Tank Bn., while the 3rd Battalion, 359th Infantry occupied the town of Bonvillers and placed roadblocks on the road from Audun to Langres.

At 0935, the commander of Stossgruppe 1 requested permission to withdraw. This was granted, and Stossgruppe 1 was promised the support of Stossgruppe 2, which had yet to encounter any US forces. This column soon ran into the 1st Battalion, 357th Infantry near Avril, supported by a platoon of towed 3-in. anti-tank guns. An attack by panzer grenadiers supported by armor was quickly broken up after two Pz IV/70 tank destroyers and two half-tracks were knocked out. The column withdrew.

Stossgruppe 1 was now trapped as the US infantry closed in. In a series of disjointed attacks, the remnants of the column were destroyed. By the end of the afternoon, Pz. Brig. 106 had been reduced to a quarter of its manpower strength, mostly in Stossgruppe 2, which had seen little

combat. A total of 764 men had been captured, including the commanders of the Panther regiment and the panzer grenadier battalions, and many more had been killed. The brigade had lost most of its equipment, including 21 of its tanks and tank destroyers, 60 of its SdKfz 250 and 251 half-tracks, and more than 100 support vehicles. Only nine of the tanks and tank destroyers of the original 47 were operational after the fighting. Over the course of the next few days, a total of 17 tanks and nine Jagdpanzer IVs were recovered or escaped back to German lines, along with a portion of the panzer grenadiers. Tactics that might have worked on the Eastern Front had proven ineffective in the west, and the brigade was largely destroyed without any appreciable effect on its intended target.

German unit records show complaints about the lack of effective reconnaissance, but Bake appears to have lost effective control of the brigade by early morning as the various columns became scattered in the hilly farmlands. US artillery forward observers reported that the Germans were suffering from communications problems, and that they could see panzer crews running from tank to tank to carry messages, even in the midst of artillery strikes. What is equally remarkable was the American reaction to the attack: the divisional history brushes off the destruction of a panzer brigade as an ordinary encounter and devotes more attention to the bloody street fighting in Thionville later in the month; in fact the fighting around Mairy essentially eliminated one of the four panzer brigades committed to the Lorraine counteroffensive.

Pz. Brig. 106 attacks Mairy, 8 September 1944, as SdKfz 251 Ausf. D armored half-tracks of the Pz. Gren. Bn. 106 move down the road towards Mairy.

Further south, a shallow bridgehead over the Moselle was made by the 5th Inf. Div. at Dornot on 8 September but was stopped in the shadow of Fort St. Blaise. In the face of intense German pressure from the 17th SS Panzer Grenadier Division, it was finally withdrawn on 11 September, but by this time, a broader and more useful bridgehead had been seized opposite Arnaville. Engineers attempting to erect a bridge across the Moselle to support the bridgehead faced a difficult time as the river was in range of German artillery less than three miles north, at Fort Driant. On 13 September, the Fort Driant artillery sank a ferrying raft, partially demolished the treadway at the river ford, and broke up a pontoon bridge that was nearly completed. Patton hoped that the 7th Armd. Div. could still push across the river to the south of the fortress city, and envelope it by a drive to the north-east. However, the 7th Armd. Div. attack stalled due to stiff German resistance, the timely destruction of key bridges, the effective use of fortifications, and the onset of rainy weather which lessened the mobility of the tanks in the slippery clay mud.

Tony Bryan 03/00

ACROSS THE MOSELLE

hile Walker's XX Corps was bogged down in its efforts to
secure usable bridgeheads near Metz, Eddy's XII Corps was
having more success around the other major Moselle river city,
the provincial capital at Nancy. Eddy decided against a direct attack on
Nancy. The city was not fortified, but the Forêt de Haye and the heights
of the Grand Couronne on the city's western approaches would make it
a difficult objective. Instead, the intention was to secure crossings north
and south of Nancy and attempt a concentric envelopment. North of
Nancy, a regimental combat team from the 80th Inf. Div. tried to take
control of a crossing near Pont-à-Mousson on 5 September. Although a
bridgehead was seized, a counterattack by the 3rd Panzer Grenadier
Division overwhelmed the small force. The Germans still held the west
bank of the Moselle at many points, and for the next few days, the 80th
Inf. Div. attempted to push them over to the east bank in preparation for
river crossing operations. The defense by the 92nd Luftwaffe Field
Regiment and 3rd Parachute Regiment was tenacious, and the German
troops did not withdraw until 10 September.

The difficulties of the 80th Inf. Div. north of Nancy prompted Eddy
to shift his emphasis south of the city using the 35th Inf. Div. The plan
was to inject the 4th Armd. Div. to envelope Nancy once the bridgehead
was gained. This decision was a controversial one, since the area south of
the city was laced with additional rivers and canals. The attack was
launched on 10 September, and 134th Infantry Regiment managed to

The 134th Infantry, 35th Division
ford across the Madon River at
Pierreville, five miles from the
Moselle. Curiously enough, the
regiment's 57mm anti-tank guns
are being carried in their 3/4 ton
trucks rather than being towed.
(US Army)

The first successful crossing of the Moselle was conducted by the 137th Infantry, 35th Division, which overcame the defensive positions of the 104th Pz. Gren. Rgt. at Neuviller-sur-Moselle, south of Bayon, late on the afternoon of 11 September. The engineers later erected a pontoon treadway bridge at the site, and it is seen here the following day with an M10 tank destroyer crossing. (US Army)

An artillery forward observer team huddles in a small stone farm building at Pont St. Vincent on 11 September 1944 during the river crossing operations near Bayon. The 134th Infantry held the left flank of the river crossing operation at Pont St. Vincent, where the Madon River runs into the Moselle. (US Army)

push a battalion across an undamaged bridge in the early evening. The Germans attempted to bomb the bridge, and finally succeeded in dropping the span with artillery in the early morning hours of 11 September. A counterattack by elements of the 15th Panzer Grenadier Division crushed the bridgehead. In the meantime, the 137th Infantry seized several other small bridgeheads during the course of the day. The 4th Armd. Div.'s CCB (Combat Command B) made its own attempt near Bayon, and the tanks of the 8th Tank Bn. managed to create their own crossing over the Bayon Canal and four streams of the Moselle. On the evening of 11/12 September, the 137th Infantry linked up with the armor near Lorey. A battalion from the 15th Panzer Grenadier Division attempted a counterattack with tank support, but was trapped and destroyed.

On Wednesday 12 September, both Hodges and Patton were called to Bradley's headquarters at Dreux. The supply situation had again reached a critical point, and Bradley warned his subordinate commanders that it would inevitably mean a slow-down in operations. Hodges estimated that he had supplies for ten more days of strenuous fighting, and the following day his 7th Corps broke across the German frontier on the way to Aachen. Patton estimated he had four days of ammunition, but enough fuel to "roll on to the Rhine" after having captured some German stocks. Bradley warned Patton that he would only have two more days to cross the Moselle in force in the Nancy-Metz region, and that if he was unable to do so, the Third Army would have to go over to the defensive from Nancy to the Luxembourg border. While fuel deliveries to the Third Army had averaged 400,000 gallons through the second week of September, by late September, they would fall to 270,000 gallons, in spite of the addition of another corps.

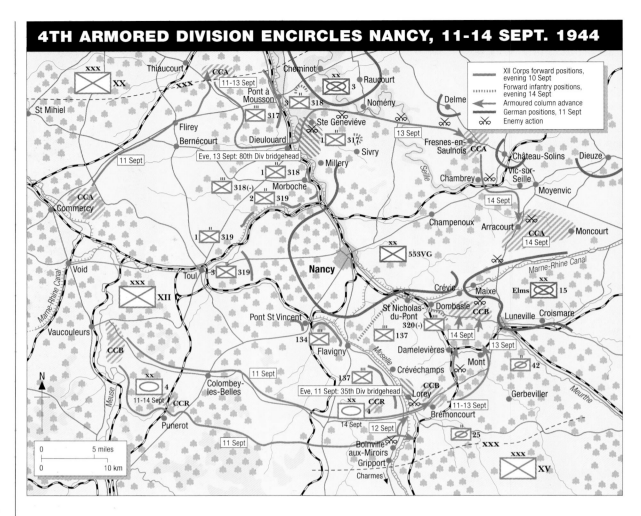

With Walker's XX Corps tied down on the approaches to Metz, Patton placed his hopes on XII Corps and the hard-charging 4th Armd. Div. The supply line had again been stretched, and the situation now reached a critical point; Bradley warned Patton that Montgomery was pressing for a higher priority of resources to the northern 21st Army Group, and that supplies would likely become scarcer. The meeting led Patton to press Eddy to complete the encirclement of Nancy.

With the bridgeheads south of Nancy secured, Eddy's XII Corps put more effort into taking northern bridgeheads. After being rebuffed near Pont-à-Mousson, his attention shifted to a crossing site near Dieulouard. Like many of the sites along this stretch of the river, this crossing was overlooked by a plateau. The military significance of the crossing site was obvious from the remains of Celtic earthworks, a Roman fort, and a medieval church-fortress. Before dawn on 11 September, two battalions from the 80th Inf. Div. crossed the river and took the high ground overlooking the river. The Germans counterattacked at 0100 on 13 September with a battalion from the 3rd Panzer Grenadier Division backed by ten StuG III assault guns. In a vicious night-time battle, the attack pushed the GIs back to within 100 yards of the bridges by 0500, but in the meantime, a company of M4 medium tanks from the

Tankers of the 8th Tank Bn., CCB, 4th Armd. Div. found some suitable fords across the Bayon canal and so were able to cross without bridges. The 8th Tank Bn. used foliage camouflage much more extensively than other tank battalions of the 4th Armd. Div., as is evident on this M4 medium tank. (US Army)

An M4A1 medium tank of the 8th Tank Bn. crosses the Bayon canal through a shallow but muddy ford on 12 September 1944. The crossing was made possible when a tank platoon used their 75mm guns to reduce the steep banks of the canal on the opposite shore. (US Army)

702nd Tank Bn. had moved forward, engaging the German armor at a range of only 200 meters. The bridgehead came very close to being overrun, but the area near the crossing site was stoutly defended by the engineers who had erected the bridges. In the face of growing American resistance, the German attack lost its momentum.

Prior to the German counterattack, Maj. Gen. John P. Wood of the 4th Armd. Div. had decided to push the CCA over the river at Dieulouard to begin the second arm of the envelopment of Nancy started by CCB near Bayon. At the head were the M8 armored cars of D Troop, 25th Cavalry Recon. Squadron, which reached the western end of the bridges around 0400 while the fighting on the east bank was going on. The regulating officer would not let the cavalry across until 0615 because of concerns about artillery coordination. After crossing the bridge, the armored cars fought their way through the German infantry before finally being forced to stop by some entrenched StuG III assault guns. A council of war had formed on the west bank, including the corps commander, Gen. Eddy, and the CCA commander, Col. Bruce Clarke. Eddy had some doubts as to whether it was sensible to deploy a large mechanized force in such a small bridgehead, especially in light of the unexpectedly fierce German attack. Clarke turned to the pugnacious commander of the 37th Tank Bn., Lt. Col. Creighton Abrams, who replied, "That's the shortest way home!" So the exploitation phase began in spite of the German action.

The German defensive line in the sector was thin, and CCA bulldozed its way through the attacking German infantry near Dieulouard with few losses. Once past the German main line of resistance, the tanks raced deep into the enemy rear towards Chateau-Salins, destroying 12 German armored vehicles, 85 other vehicles, and some artillery in the process. By the end of the day, the armored force was deep behind German lines and threatening to complete the envelopment of Nancy. The division log noted, "The rapid drive of

The 8th Tank Bn. crossing of the Bayon Canal was made possible by the low water level in several sections. This is evident here as several of the barges are left high and dry in the mud. The M4 exiting the canal is one of the newer M4 medium tanks armed with the long 76mm gun. These were not in widespread service in the 4th Armd. Div. at the time, since Patton did not feel that they were necessary. (US Army)

CCA through the enemy lines has so disrupted the enemy forces that small groups have been apprehended wandering, almost aimlessly, through their bivouac areas."

The German response

Blaskowitz recognized the threat posed by this armored breakthrough and began moving forces forward to crush the bridgehead and cut off CCA. Intense fighting raged in the forests and on the hills near the bridgeheads as the 3rd and 15th Pz. Gren. Div. attacked in force over the next two days. These attacks were repulsed by the 80th Inf. Div., and by 16 September, the Germans had suffered too many casualties to continue the fight. Rather than risk losing the substantial forces trapped in Nancy, Blaskowitz gave permission for units in Nancy to begin to

The Wehrmacht responded to the Bayon crossing by a series of counterattacks, including a brief tank attack by PzKpfw IVs of the 15th Panzer Grenadier Division near Mehoncourt, in which one M4 medium tank of the 8th Tank Bn. was knocked out. It can be seen in the background while a medic tends to a wounded tanker in the foreground. (US Army)

The northern crossing of the Moselle took place near the town of Dieulouard. The area is laced with small tributaries of the Moselle which complicated the crossing. Here an M4 bulldozer tank is used to create a roadway across a narrow tributary of the river on 12 September. (US Army)

Troops of the 80th Inf. Div. cross the Moselle near Dieulouard on 12 September via an improvised bridge. The next day, the engineers had erected a pontoon treadway bridge elsewhere on the river to enable heavy traffic to cross. (US Army)

evacuate on the evening of 13 September, and the loss of the bridgeheads at Dieulouard and Bayon led to the complete abandonment of the city over the next few days. It was occupied by the 80th Inf. Div. with the support of the FFI French resistance forces on 15 September.

Plans for Hitler's panzer offensive in Lorraine had been steadily delayed through the first two weeks of September. His original scheme had been to launch the attack from the area of Pontarlier on the Swiss border north-west towards the Plateau de Langres, cutting off US forces advancing towards the Belfort Gap and preventing a link-up of the US Third and Seventh Armies. The attack would have involved three panzer grenadier divisions and three panzer brigades, with three more panzer divisions and three more panzer brigades as reinforcements. An initial attack date had been set for 12 September, but this had proved

LEFT, TOP **The Dieulouard bridgehead was the scene of intense fighting in the early morning hours of 13 September as the 3rd Panzer Grenadier Division attempted to crush it. The bridgehead was held, and served as the springboard for CCA, 4th Armd. Div.'s drive on Arracourt. Here, German prisoners pass through the town later in the day, after the attack had been beaten back. (US Army)**

LEFT, BELOW **The destruction of bridges can slow but not stop a river crossing if the opponent is prepared. Here an M4 crosses the Moselle on a treadway bridge, while in the background, the destroyed local bridge can be seen. The commander of the CCA, 4th Armd. Div., Col. Bruce Clarke, had been instrumental in the development and fielding of engineer bridging for US armored units before the war. (US Army)**

impossible, and by the second week of September, the German retreat and the approach of the two US armies near Dijon, overrunning the areas from which the offensive would have been staged, had disabled Hitler's plans still further.

On 10 September, Manteuffel was again called to the Führer headquarters. Hitler's revised plan envisioned an attack from the Plateau de Langres and Epinal towards Reims, with an aim towards cutting off Patton's Third Army when it was entangled in the battles along the Moselle River. The American advances threatened to create a breach between the German First and Nineteenth Armies which would allow the American tank columns to race ahead into the Saar basin across the German frontier. Although the notional aim of the counteroffensive was to cut off the Third Army, the more realistic officers at Blaskowitz's

RIGHT **The bridgeheads south of Metz in the XX Corps sector proved even more difficult than those around Nancy, with the crossing sites under fire from the artillery of Fort Driant. On 12 September, a heavy bridge was finally completed near Arnaville, allowing the 7th Armd. Div.'s CCB to send reinforcements to the beleaguered infantry on the west bank. This is an M32 armored recovery vehicle crossing the bridge on 13 September. (US Army)**

BELOW, RIGHT **The Germans destroyed most of the bridges over the Moselle. However, in the days following the first crossings, engineers began to use the pilings of the bridges to create improvised crossings, like the one at Arnaville in use by medical teams on 21 September. (US Army)**

headquarters hoped that the attack would at least prevent a rupture between the First and Nineteenth Armies and cover the Vosges mountain area while a new "Vosges Outpost" defensive line was created.

Manteuffel arrived at Army Group G headquarters on 11 September and was briefed on the local situation. Fifth Panzer Army existed more in Hitler's imagination than in reality, and Manteuffel felt that the counteroffensive plan was "beyond all hope." To make matters worse, the US First Army attacking from Belgium were approaching Aachen, the first major German city to be threatened on the Western Front. Rundstedt was stripping forces from all over the theater to reinforce this sector. Two of the panzer brigades slated for the Lorraine offensive, Panzer Brigades 107 and 108, were being sent towards Aachen instead,

ABOVE **With the CCB of 4th Armd. Div. and 35th Infantry over the Moselle, the tanks began moving on to encircle the regional capital of Nancy. Here, an M4 medium tank of the 737th Tank Bn. fires on buildings near Dombasle, along the left flank of the advance on 15 September 1944, in support of the 320th Infantry, which was crossing a nearby canal at the time. (US Army)**

LEFT **A couple of GIs of the 35th Inf. Div. enjoy coffee and donuts at a Red Cross station outside Nancy on 19 September 1944. Task Force Sebree from the division entered the city on 15 September and found that it had been abandoned by the Germans. (US Army)**

The fighting during late September 1944 in Lorraine was characterized by rain and mud. It was one of the wettest Septembers on record, and the fields soon turned to glutinous mud, as shown here with a jeep from the 134th Infantry, 35th Division near Nancy. (US Army)

and the date for the offensive was postponed to 15 September. However, Hitler was adamant that it should start no later than that, even if only some of the allotted forces were ready.

The units assigned to the Fifth Panzer Army included: the 21st Panzer Division from OB-West's reserve, which was refitting in Molsheim; the 15th Panzer Grenadier Division, which was already heavily committed to the fighting in the First Army sector; and Panzer Brigades 106, 111, 112, and 113. The Fifth Panzer Army was organized into the 47th Panzer Corps headquartered at Remiremont, and the 57th Panzer Corps, activated on 18 September, at Languimberg. Command and control of the army was made more difficult by the fact that it did not control its own sector of the front, sharing control with the First and Nineteenth Armies. There were not enough telephone lines to support separate headquarters, and the Fifth Panzer Army took a back-seat to the existing formations. After the decimation of Pz. Brig. 106 in the attack on 90th Inf. Div., Hitler ordered that none of the units intended for his offensive be used for frontal attacks on the Americans but only for the planned counterattack. However, before Hitler's revised plan could be put into effect, Allied attacks in a new sector threatened the staging area for the panzer attack.

DISASTER AT DOMPAIRE

hile Hodges' and Eddy's corps fought for the Moselle bridgeheads, Patton's Third Army was reinforced by a third corps, Maj. Gen. Wade Haislip's XV Corps. This had been taken from the Third Army during the Seine crossing operation and was being returned to Patton's forces in Lorraine to cover his exposed right flank. During the push into Lorraine, the right flank had been ignored due to the weakness of the Wehrmacht. But in the meantime, the 6th Army Group was advancing northward after its landings in southern France and was already moving up along the Swiss border towards the Belfort Gap. As the 6th Army Group closed on Third Army, German forces would be pushed forward into the gap between the two Allied armies, requiring more attention to the flank. A patrol from the French 2nd Armored Division, the southernmost unit in XV Corps, linked up with a patrol from the 6th Army Group late on 10 September to the west of Dijon, marking a continuous line of Allied forces from the North Sea to the Mediterranean.

On 11 September, Haislip's XV Corps began moving forward to push the weak German 64th Corps back over the Moselle. The spearhead of XV Corps was the French 2nd Armored Division, commanded by the legendary Jacques Leclerc. This division was the first Free French division formed, and the only one to operate separately from de Lattre's 1st French Army in the 6th Army Group. The division had originally served under Haislip's XV Corps in Normandy. Leclerc had appreciated

Mines were a constant menace and accounted for about a quarter of the US tanks knocked out during the war. This M4 (76mm) of the 749th Tank Bn. was disabled near Charmes on 12 September during the fighting between the US 79th Division and the German 16th Infantry Division. While the US forces kept the Germans occupied, the French 2nd Armored Division sent a combat command deep behind German lines, precipitating the tank battle at Dompaire. (US Army)

ABOVE **The French controlled the high ground over Dompaire during the fighting. This is a panoramic view from the hills above Damas, with Dompaire at the base of the hill to the left and Lamerey to the right. Most of the tank fighting took place in view of this location. (S. Zaloga)**

RIGHT **A Panther Ausf. G tank lies in ruins in the streets of Dompaire, following the battle with the French 2nd Armored Division. A significant number of the tanks lost during the battle were credited to P-47 Thunderbolts of the XIX TAC, which conducted four attack missions over the town during the fighting. (US Air Force)**

the aggressive command style of the French-speaking Haislip, but had had problems when shifted to Maj. Gen. L. T. Gerow's V Corps for the liberation of Paris. De Gaulle had wanted Leclerc's division to remain in Paris as a counterweight to the Communist-dominated resistance, or transferred to de Lattre's 1st French Corps, but Leclerc had been unhappy being subordinated to a former Vichy general like de Lattre and had finally won permission to return to Haislip's XV Corps. Haislip had been equally pleased, as Leclerc's division was easily the best of the Free French divisions, being composed mostly of volunteers from the tough African colonial units. While the US 79th Inf. Div. pinned the German 16th Inf. Div. by frontal attack, the French 2nd Armored Division sent its GTL (*Groupement Tactique Langlade*, Combat Command Langlade) through the gap between the weak Kampfgruppe

The RBFM (*Régiment Blindé de Fusiliers Marins*, Armored Regiment of Naval Riflemen) was the tank destroyer battalion of the French 2nd Armored Division. Its platoons were usually spread out among the various battle-groups to provide added firepower to the tank companies when encountering German Panthers. The battalion was formed in North Africa in 1943 from volunteers from the French fleet, and the crews retained their sailor's cap. Here, French Minister of the Navy Jacquinot visits crews who distinguished themselves during the fighting at Dompaire. (US Army)

RIGHT *Siroco*, an M10 of the 3rd Platoon, 4th Squadron of the RBFM, was the highest scoring tank destroyer of the battalion, credited with nine German tanks including three Panthers at Dompaire. The tank destroyers were named after pre-war French warships. *Siroco* was preserved after the war and is currently on display at the Saumur tank museum in the Loire region of France, near the French Army cavalry school. (S. Zaloga)

Ottenbacher and the 16th Inf. Div. (The French combat commands were named after their leader, in this case, Col. Paul Girot de Langlade.)

The French armored columns were soon behind the German positions and threatened to encircle them. In spite of Hitler's orders to conserve the panzer brigades for the planned offensive, Blaskowitz felt it was more important to keep the defensive line intact than hoard precious tank formations for a doomed offensive. He ordered Manteuffel to send some of his forces into the area west of Epinal to prevent the collapse of the entire 64th Corps. The plan was to use Col. von Usedom's Pz. Brig. 112 and a combat group of the 21st Panzer Division to clear out the rear areas of the French intruders. The panzer brigade moved out of Epinal in two groups: the Panthers of I/Pz. Rgt. 29 reached the town of Dompaire in the early evening of 12 September and the PzKpfw IV tanks of Pz. Rgt. 2112 moved towards Darney.

GTL Langlade had excellent intelligence about the strength and location of the German forces from the local French villagers. By late evening of 12 September, I/Pz. Rgt. 29 was strung out in a poorly chosen bivouac in a shallow valley from the village of Dompaire to the west and through its neighboring hamlets of Lamerey and Madonne to the east. Langlade decided to attack this formation first, even though it was larger than his own forces.

GTL Langlade consisted of mechanized infantry from the *Régiment de Marche du Tchade* (RMT) and companies from two tank battalions, the 12e *Régiment de Chasseurs d'Afrique* (RCA), and the 501e *Régiment de Chars de Combat* (RCC). Langlade's force was composed of three battlegroups: Group Putz near Darney, and Groups Massu and Minjonnet near Dompaire. Each group had 15 M4A2 medium tanks with 75mm guns,

one M4A2 with a 76mm gun, three to four M10 tank destroyers, and one or two companies of infantry. The total strength of GTL Langlade was inferior to Pz. Brig. 112, at less than half the number of tanks and infantry, but Langlade had the advantage of better positions, as well as artillery and air support which the Germans lacked completely.

Group Massu took up positions in the hills overlooking Dompaire from the west and north-west, and Group Minjonnet towards the center of the town, with clear fields of fire to the east. Group Massu was the first to encounter the Germans: during a probe towards Dompaire on the evening of 12 September, they had a short firefight with Panther tanks on the south-western side of the town. The French M4 tanks withdrew into the woods above the town after each side had lost a tank.

The terrain held by the French was a plateau a few kilometers south of Dompaire, separated by gradually sloping farm fields and scattered woods. This provided excellent fields of fire against the town below and clear vantage points from which to direct artillery fire. The French troops were more experienced and better trained than their German adversaries. For example, the 12e RCA, previously commanded by Langlade, had fought against the Afrika Korps in the Tunisian campaign on Somua S-35 tanks before being re-equipped and retrained by the US Army in 1943-44 on M4A2 tanks. The other units had been drawn mostly from French-African units. Curiously enough, the M10 tank destroyers were manned by volunteer sailors from the RBFM (Armored Regiment of Naval Riflemen).

Like most other panzer brigades, Pz. Brig. 112 was new, poorly trained, and untested in combat. A French villager who watched the column of Panthers move through Lamerey towards Dompaire the evening before the battle recalled that the crews "seemed almost like children." The French expected the Germans to conduct rigorous night patrols to reconnoiter their positions. Instead, the Germans sat out the rainy night in comfort in the villages while the French endured the rain in muddy farm fields, preparing for the next day's battle. A German officer who participated in the battle later recalled that before the battle, the Germans had seriously underestimated the combat skills of the French tankers.

The fighting began along the eastern side of the town. Panther tanks began to try to infiltrate south out of Lamerey by using the hilly terrain and woods. A pair of M10 tank destroyers in hull-down position stopped the initial advance, further emphasizing the point by calling in an artillery strike of 250 rounds from a battery of 105mm howitzers. Group Minjonnet sent a company of light tanks towards Damas, to the south of Dompaire, to try to force out entrenched German infantry, and faced a stiff fight.

The previous night, Langlade had arranged to receive American air support, and around 0800, Col. Tower, the TALO (tactical air liaison officer) from the XIX TAC, moved up in a radio-equipped M4 tank to the command post of Group Massu in the hills above Dompaire. He directed an air strike from P-47s of the 406th Fighter-Bomber Group against the Panther tanks strung out in the hamlets of Lamerey and Madonne. The I/Pz. Rgt. 29 was raked with rocket fire, bombs, and machine-guns; the Germans responded with ineffective 20mm fire. A French tanker recalled that it was "the most impressive and terrifying

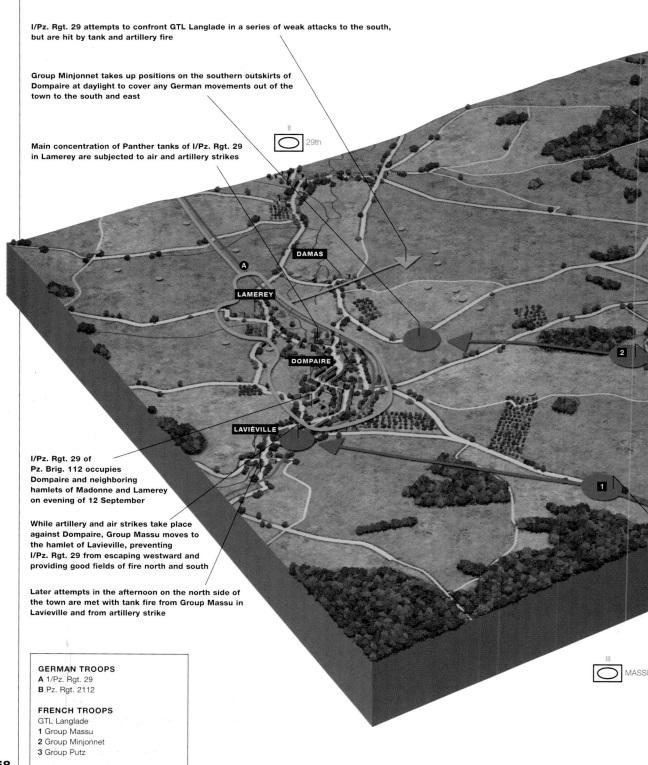

I/Pz. Rgt. 29 attempts to confront GTL Langlade in a series of weak attacks to the south, but are hit by tank and artillery fire

Group Minjonnet takes up positions on the southern outskirts of Dompaire at daylight to cover any German movements out of the town to the south and east

II
29th

Main concentration of Panther tanks of I/Pz. Rgt. 29 in Lamerey are subjected to air and artillery strikes

DAMAS

A

LAMEREY

DOMPAIRE

LAVIÉVILLE

2

1

I/Pz. Rgt. 29 of Pz. Brig. 112 occupies Dompaire and neighboring hamlets of Madonne and Lamerey on evening of 12 September

While artillery and air strikes take place against Dompaire, Group Massu moves to the hamlet of Lavieville, preventing I/Pz. Rgt. 29 from escaping westward and providing good fields of fire north and south

Later attempts in the afternoon on the north side of the town are met with tank fire from Group Massu in Lavieville and from artillery strike

III
MASSU

GERMAN TROOPS
A 1/Pz. Rgt. 29
B Pz. Rgt. 2112

FRENCH TROOPS
GTL Langlade
1 Group Massu
2 Group Minjonnet
3 Group Putz

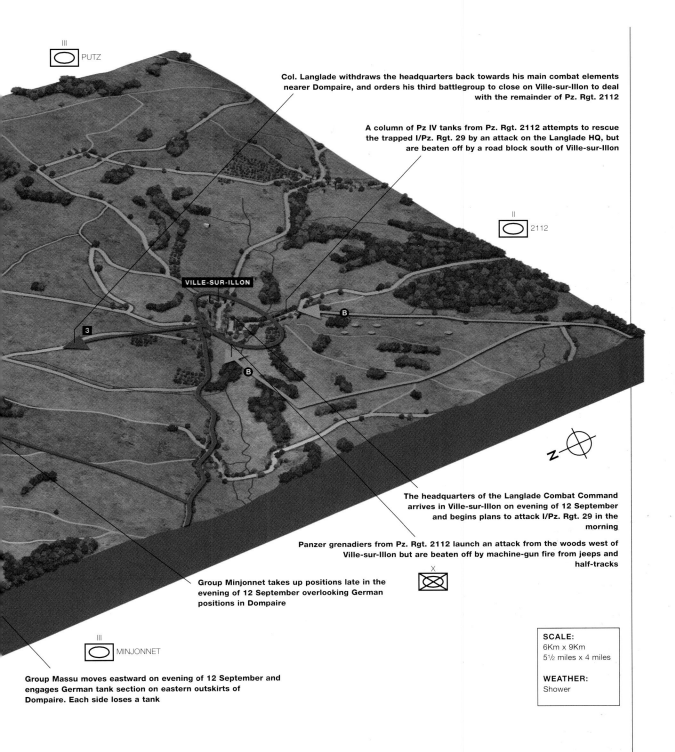

PUTZ

Col. Langlade withdraws the headquarters back towards his main combat elements nearer Dompaire, and orders his third battlegroup to close on Ville-sur-Illon to deal with the remainder of Pz. Rgt. 2112

A column of Pz IV tanks from Pz. Rgt. 2112 attempts to rescue the trapped I/Pz. Rgt. 29 by an attack on the Langlade HQ, but are beaten off by a road block south of Ville-sur-Illon

2112

VILLE-SUR-ILLON

3

B

B

The headquarters of the Langlade Combat Command arrives in Ville-sur-Illon on evening of 12 September and begins plans to attack I/Pz. Rgt. 29 in the morning

Panzer grenadiers from Pz. Rgt. 2112 launch an attack from the woods west of Ville-sur-Illon but are beaten off by machine-gun fire from jeeps and half-tracks

Group Minjonnet takes up positions late in the evening of 12 September overlooking German positions in Dompaire

MINJONNET

Group Massu moves eastward on evening of 12 September and engages German tank section on eastern outskirts of Dompaire. Each side loses a tank

X

SCALE:
6Km x 9Km
5½ miles x 4 miles

WEATHER:
Shower

THE DESTRUCTION OF PANZER BRIGADE 112 AT DOMPAIRE, 13 SEPTEMBER 1944

GTL Langlade encircled the weak German units to prevent a counter-offensive and severely reduced the German panzer force.

Following the defeat of Pz. Brig. 112 at Dompaire, the US 79th Inf. Div. in concert with the French 2nd Armored Division began an assault across the Mortagne River. The 314th Infantry pushed through the town of Gerbeviller on 20 September, after Manteuffel had ordered the weakened 21st Panzer Division and Pz. Brig. 112 to withdraw eastward. (US Army)

spectacle imaginable." The French observers estimated that eight tanks had been knocked out, but the smoke and fire in the villages made it difficult to be precise. Under the cover of the air attack, the French columns began moving into position to trap the Germans in the villages and prevent their movement down neighboring roads. French M4 medium tanks entered the west side of Dompaire through the hamlet of Lavieville and moved up the hill towards Bouzemont to take up positions on the hills behind the Germans. They were followed later in the morning by a platoon of M10 tank destroyers. The Panthers were now hemmed in on three sides.

Around 1100 a second flight of six P-47 Thunderbolts arrived overhead, this time in bright sunlight and clear skies. There was some confusion due to the infiltration of French tanks into the villages, and the German use of Allied air recognition panels on some of their tanks. After consultation with the TALO, the air strike commenced. French villagers later reported that the strike had terrified the inexperienced German tank crews and that a number of crews had deserted and tried to steal civilian clothes in order to escape. The commander of I/Pz. Rgt. 29 requested assistance from the brigade's other tank battalion, Pz. Rgt. 2112 in Darney, when it became clear that the Germans were trapped.

Langlade's command post was in the village of Ville-sur-Illon, on the plateau south of Dompaire. Around 1330, he received a phone call from a woman in an outlying house south of his position warning him that she had seen 300-400 German panzer grenadiers and some tanks moving towards the town. This was the spearhead of the rescue party from Pz. Rgt. 2112 that had been requested a few hours earlier. The force consisted of a battalion of panzer grenadiers and a number of the regiment's 45 PzKpfw IV tanks, and the advance posed a serious risk to the entire French battlegroup. It not only threatened to overrun the French command post, but it could also sandwich Group Minjonnet against the German tanks in Dompaire. However, the German infantry halted abruptly after finding and drinking a large cache of kirsch liquor in a garage along the route. In the meantime, Langlade organized a hasty defense of his command post by setting up a roadblock along route D6 using a handful of tanks, M10 destroyers, and towed anti-tank guns.

About a dozen PzKpfw IV tanks moved within range of the roadblock. The lead two were destroyed by M4 medium tanks at 200-300 meters, and three more were wiped out later by concealed M10 tank destroyers. The German infantry, delayed by their earlier drinking, finally arrived from the west against the right flank of the French position. This area was defended by only two jeeps armed with .30 caliber machine-guns. They opened fire, and then boldly raced out into the forest clearing, raking the panzer grenadiers with machine-guns. This put a temporary halt to this threat as the German troops retreated into the nearby woods. A pair of half-tracks from an engineer platoon were rushed in to assist and managed to capture a few prisoners. When the size of the German force became evident from prisoner interrogations, Langlade evacuated his command post to more defensible positions closer to the bulk of his battlegroup near Dompaire.

While the fighting was taking place on the plateau, at 1530 a third air strike by a flight of six P-47s began against Lamerey. This attack was partly wasted on burnt-out tanks due to difficulties in establishing a radio link with the TALO. The I/Pz. Rgt. 29 in Dompaire staged a series of weak, intermittent attacks through the afternoon, usually consisting of two or three Panthers trying to find weak points in the French positions. This was a futile exercise as the French had carefully established camouflaged hull-down positions around the village and were able to destroy the more heavily armored Panthers with flank shots at close range. One probe in the early afternoon nearly found a gap, in a position protected only by an exposed 57mm towed anti-tank gun, but a barrage from a battery of 105mm howitzers put an end to the attack. German prisoners made it quite clear that they feared the artillery even more than the air strikes. Due to the excellent observation positions

A German casualty is evacuated by a stretcher team from the 45th Division near Archettes after the 7th Army crossed the Moselle near Arches on 21 September. One of the stretcher bearers is a German prisoner-of-war. (US Army)

afforded by the plateau, the French were able to bring down precision artillery strikes all day long, regardless of the changing weather, and a fourth air strike around 1500 left many of the Panthers in the hamlets east of Dompaire burnt or abandoned.

After a day of weak and futile probes against the plateau to the south and east, I/Pz. Rgt. 29 began to stage an attack to the north-east, towards the French blocking positions on the hills behind Dompaire. An initial foray of three Panthers proved half-hearted after the lead vehicle was struck ineffectively at 1,600 meters by M10 fire. Two more platoons of Panthers, accompanied by panzer grenadiers, appeared next. Several were put out of action by the M10 tank destroyers. This temporarily broke up the attack, which resumed about 1830 for the loss of two more Panthers. By evening, the attacks had petered out, and by the end of the day, Pz. Brig. 112 was a shambles. The I/Pz. Rgt. 29 had been virtually wiped out, losing 34 of its Panther tanks and having only four operational. Pz. Rgt. 2112 had only 17 of its original 45 Pz. Kpfw IV tanks operational and had lost many infantry in the woods near Ville-sur-Illon.

The following morning, Group Massu occupied the eastern end of Dompaire, finding four abandoned Panther tanks in the streets of the town. A Kampfgruppe, made up mostly of the 192nd Pz. Gren. Rgt. under Col. von Luck from the 21st Panzer Division, was sent west from Epinal to reinforce the attack, but by the time it arrived, on 14 September, Langlade had been reinforced near Ville-sur-Illon by his third battlegroup, Group Putz. Von Luck's battlegroup, consisting of 17 tanks and 240 infantry, made an attack on Group Minjonnet from the east, near Hennecourt, attempting to prevent the complete annihilation of 1/Pz. Rgt. 29 in Dompaire. It was brought under fire by divisional artillery and stopped after an hour of fighting. The German 47th Panzer Corps headquarters decided that any further attacks would be futile. Von Luck and the surviving elements of Pz. Brig. 112 were ordered to withdraw towards positions west of Epinal, hoping that these remnants might be used later in the planned counteroffensive. The hapless survivors of Pz. Brig. 112 were put under 21st Panzer Division command. In less than two days of fighting, the brigade had been reduced to only 21 operational tanks of its original 90. Casualties were estimated to be 350 dead and about 1,000 wounded. Of the 33 tanks found in Group Massu's sector, 13 had been knocked out by tank or tank-destroyer fire, 16 by aircraft attack, and four had been abandoned intact. French losses were five M4A2 medium tanks, two M5A1 light tanks, two half-tracks and two jeeps; 44 were killed, and a single P-47 was shot down.

The decimation of Pz. Brig. 112 on 13 September, less than a week after the defeat of Pz. Brig. 106, substantially reduced the tank strength available to Manteuffel for the planned counteroffensive. Fifth Panzer Army was now down to only two panzer brigades, the demoralized remnants of brigades 112 and 106, and the understrength and tank-less 21st Panzer Division. By the night of 17 September, the German 64th Corps had collapsed and had retreated over the Moselle, with most of the 16th Inf. Div., trapped by the Americans and French. All of Patton's three corps were now lined up along the Moselle. On 19 September, Haislip's XV Corps crossed the river and advanced towards the Mortagne River, reaching the area south of Luneville.

THE TANK BATTLES FOR ARRACOURT

The American and French advances in the XV Corps sector forced Blaskowitz to inform Rundstedt that the proposed panzer counteroffensive along the west side of the Moselle was no longer feasible since the Wehrmacht had lost the Plateau de Langres from which it was to be launched. Not wishing to display a lack of the "offensive spirit" that Hitler took to be a measure of loyalty to the regime, Blaskowitz suggested a more feasible, though more limited, offensive. This would emanate from the Epinal area to the north-east, seize a base of operations at Luneville, and then cut off the lead elements of Patton's armored spearhead, the 4th Armd. Div., around Arracourt. Blaskowitz planned to use the Fifth Panzer Army attack to accomplish the more limited tactical objective of closing the gap between the First and Nineteenth Armies, though the plan had to be couched in more ambitious terms to mollify Hitler's predilection for the grandiose.

Rundstedt knew better than to approve the change in Hitler's plan on his own authority, so sent the proposal to OKW in Berlin. The OKW approved the plan, reinforcing Manteuffel's force with the 11th Panzer Division and noting that Panzer Brigades 107 and 108 would be added to the attack once Hitler's intuition told him it was the right moment. In fact, both brigades were committed later to the Aachen fighting instead.

The panzer offensive was now scheduled to begin no later than 18 September 1944, even though it was unlikely that the 11th Panzer Division would be available. Rundstedt did win a concession from the inspector of the panzer forces on the Western Front, Gen. Lt. Horst

A column from the 106th Cavalry Group passes a PzKpfw IV with its turret blown off on a road near Luneville on 20 September. This is probably a tank from Pz. Brig. 112, which was incorporated into the 21st Panzer Division after its disaster at Dompaire and employed with little success against the XV Corps advance on Luneville a week later. (US Army)

A lieutenant from the 79th Division calls in mortar fire during the fighting around Luneville on 21 September. The city of Luneville remained a source of contention even after it was occupied by US forces since the German 15th Pz. Gren. Div. could launch attacks on it from the neighboring Parroy forest. (US Army)

Stumpff, that priority in new tanks would be given to units assigned for the attack, especially the depleted 21st Panzer Division. However, this never materialized. On 16 September, detailed orders were issued for the offensive. Manteuffel protested that the Fifth Panzer Army was not strong enough to conduct such an ambitious attack, but he was told in no uncertain terms that he would attack on 18 September regardless of his opinion.

The objectives were to eliminate the US Army XII Corps from the east bank of the Moselle by seizing Luneville as a base of operation, then crush the bridgehead at Pont-à-Mousson. The 58th Panzer Corps would attack westward along the north bank of the Marne-Rhine canal against the US 4th Armd. Div. using Pz. Brig. 113 and the 15th Panzer Grenadier Division. The 47th Panzer Corps would strike towards Luneville using

The tank fighting in late September centered around the small town of Arracourt, seen here in the upper center of an aerial photo taken shortly after the war. The most intense fighting took place around Hill 318, in the center of the photo, immediately to the right of the Benamont Woods seen on the left. In an aerial photo like this, the area appears flat, but in fact the terrain slopes downward towards the bottom of the photo, to the south-east. (David Isby)

Pz. Brig. 111, the remnants of Pz. Brig. 112, and the 21st Panzer Division.

The initial objective for Luttwitz's 47th Panzer Corps was the town of Luneville. The situation near the town was fluid. Two squadrons from "Patton's Ghosts", the 2nd Cavalry Group, had tried to enter the town on 15 September but were beaten off by elements of the 15th Pz. Gren. Div. The next day, the 42nd Cav. Sqn. again moved on Luneville, reinforced with tanks of CCR of the 4th Armd. Div. The German infantry withdrew. The 42nd Cav. Sqn. did not occupy the town, but set up a line of outposts to the south-east. On the evening of 17 September, German infantry again infiltrated the town and reported that it was in their hands. When the panzer attack began early on the morning of 18 September 1944, Luttwitz

An M18 tank destroyer from the 603rd Tank Destroyer Battalion, CCB, 7th Armd. Div. guards the intersection at Rue Carnot in Luneville, facing towards Frambois, on 22 September. Vehicles from this unit took part in the tank fighting in Luneville with Pz. Brig. 111 on 18 September. (US Army)

was under the impression that Luneville was in friendly hands. Instead, the lead column of Panther tanks from Pz. Brig. 111 ran into an outpost of the 42nd Cav. Sqn. The squadron's M8 75mm howitzer motor carriages (HMC) rushed forward to provide fire support for the lightly armed M8 armored cars. However, the little howitzers on these light armored vehicles were completely ineffective against the thick frontal armor of the Panthers. Three of the six M8 HMCs were quickly destroyed, and the German tanks pressed ahead. However, a tenacious defense by dismounted cavalry troops delayed the panzer grenadiers until 1100. The commander of the 42nd Squadron was killed and the commander of the 2nd Cavalry Group was severely wounded in the ensuing fighting. Although badly outnumbered, the cavalry force managed to delay the German advance long enough for the 2nd Cavalry Group to withdraw through Luneville and to call for reinforcements. CCA of 4th Armd. Div. rushed a task force to the scene, along with elements of CCB of the 6th Armd. Div. A close-range firefight developed

Fifth Panzer Army commander Hasso von Manteuffel had a bitter exchange with Col. Heinrich von Bronsart-Schellendorf, commander of Pz. Brig. 111, on 22 September. Schellendorf was killed by machine-gun fire during the fighting later in the day near Juvelize. (USNA)

inside the town between the 603rd Tank Destroyer Battalion and lead German armor elements. The most potent American reinforcements were two battalions of M7 105mm HMC and the 183rd Field Artillery Group which began to pummel the German troops. The intense artillery fire forced the Germans behind the rail line in the southern section of the town. Manteuffel ordered Pz. Brig. 111 to disengage from the town and proceed to Parroy for the continuation of the main attack.

At the end of the first day of the panzer offensive, the Germans had made few gains, holding on to parts of Luneville, and even before the southern thrust had accomplished much of anything, Luttwitz found that his left flank was threatened by the continuing advance of the US Army XV Corps. There was also pressure from Hitler and the OKW to press the attack. The objective was again redefined, with Nancy now being the initial objective instead of Chateau Salins, to rescue trapped German forces. (Hitler would throw away entire divisions due to careless decisions, and then become obsessed with rescuing a few encircled battalions in another sector.)

Manteuffel was forced to reorganize his plans yet again. Luttwitz was ordered to take up defensive positions using the 15th Pz. Gren. Div., 21st Pz. Div., and Pz. Brig. 112, while Pz. Brig. 111 was taken away and assigned to the 58th Panzer Corps, which would now bear the brunt of

PREPARING FOR THE ASSAULT: German panzer grenadiers climb aboard the Panther tanks and half-tracks of Pz. Brig. 113 as they prepare for their assault towards Arracourt.

Tony Bryan 03/00

Two prominent combat leaders of CCA, 4th Armd. Div. were Lt. Col. Creighton Abrams, commander of the 37th Tank Bn., seen here to the left, and Lt. Col. Harold Cohen, commander of the 10th Armored Infantry Battalion, seen to the right. The close cooperation between the tanks and half-track infantry was one of the reasons for the success of this fighting force. (J. Leach collection, Patton Museum)

the offensive mission. At midnight, Manteuffel telephoned the 58th Panzer Corps commander, Gen. Kreuger, and told him that Pz. Brig. 113 must be ready to conduct offensive operations towards Arracourt or he would suffer the direst consequences. The disorganized condition of the German panzer forces and persistent demands for action from Berlin forced Manteuffel into a ragged and piecemeal commitment of his forces. The 2nd Cavalry Group had prevented German reconnaissance units from determining much about the dispositions of the 4th Armd. Div. around Arracourt, and the Luftwaffe had also proven to be useless in this regard. Manteuffel was operating in an intelligence void, exacerbated by the tendency of the Eastern Front veterans to launch tank attacks without any scouting.

It was not immediately apparent to Patton that a major panzer offensive had begun. There was no signals intelligence on German intentions, and the attack on Luneville was so weak and disjointed that it was presumed to be a minor local action. Patton's plan for 19 September was for the 4th Armd. Div. to continue its attack towards the German border. CCB was to push from Delme towards Saabrucken, while CCA would attack from Arracourt towards Saareguemines. On the night of 18/19 September, there were numerous reports along the frontlines of the sounds of German tracked vehicles.

The early morning attack had been planned as a two-brigade assault, with Pz. Brig. 113 attacking the eastern spearhead of the CCA forces near Lezey while Pz. Brig. 111 attacked the center near Arracourt. This would have given the Germans more than a four-to-one advantage in armor in this sector. In the event, Pz. Brig. 111 became lost during the night road march, allegedly after receiving bad instructions from a French farmer, but even without Pz. Brig. 111, Pz. Brig. 113 still had more than a two-to-one advantage.

Panther Ausf. G tanks of Pz. Brig. 111 maneuver on the outskirts of Bures on 20 September. Bures was one of the small towns between the Parroy forest and the base of the Arracourt hills, and so was a favorite staging area for the German attacks. (USNA)

The morning of 19 September dawned as it had for the previous few days with a thick fog in the low-lying areas. Around 0730, Capt. W. Dwight, a liaison officer moving between his platoons in a jeep, ran into the rear of a German tank column near Moncourt. In the thick fog, he went unnoticed, and he escaped to Arracourt, reporting to the 37th Tank Bn. commander, Lt. Col. Creighton Abrams, by radio. An outpost of M5A1 light tanks from Company D, 37th Tank Bn. encountered the same group, but were able to withdraw in the thick fog and report back.

The German column was a company of Panther tanks spearheading the eastern column of the Pz. Brig. 113 attack. A platoon of M4 medium tanks from Co. C, 37th Tank Bn. were holding an outpost when they heard the lead tanks moving towards their position. A group of Panther tanks emerged from the fog about 75 yards from their position. Quickly engaging them, three Panthers were knocked out in rapid succession. In shock, the German column broke off to the south-west. The US tankers enjoyed a greater familiarity with the local terrain, and Capt. Lamison raced a platoon of M4 medium tanks to a commanding ridge west of Bezange-la-Petite to trap the withdrawing panzer column. As the eight surviving Panthers appeared, four were quickly knocked out at close range from the flanks. Before the Germans could respond, the M4 tanks moved behind the cover of the reverse slopes. In the dense fog, the Panther crews had no idea where the American tanks were located, and seconds later, the M4 tanks reappeared from behind the ridge and destroyed the remaining four Panthers.

In the meantime, Capt. Dwight had reached Arracourt and was ordered to take a platoon of M18 tank destroyers to reinforce the outpost near

BELOW Lt. Col. Creighton Abrams, commander of 37th Tank Bn., is seen here on his command tank named Thunderbolt. During the fighting in 1944/45, Abrams had seven different tanks named Thunderbolt, losing them to enemy fire or mechanical exhaustion. He was probably one of the highest scoring US tankers of World War II, but the total number of enemy tanks knocked out by his crew is not known as he did not consider such tallies significant. (J. Leach collection, Patton Museum)

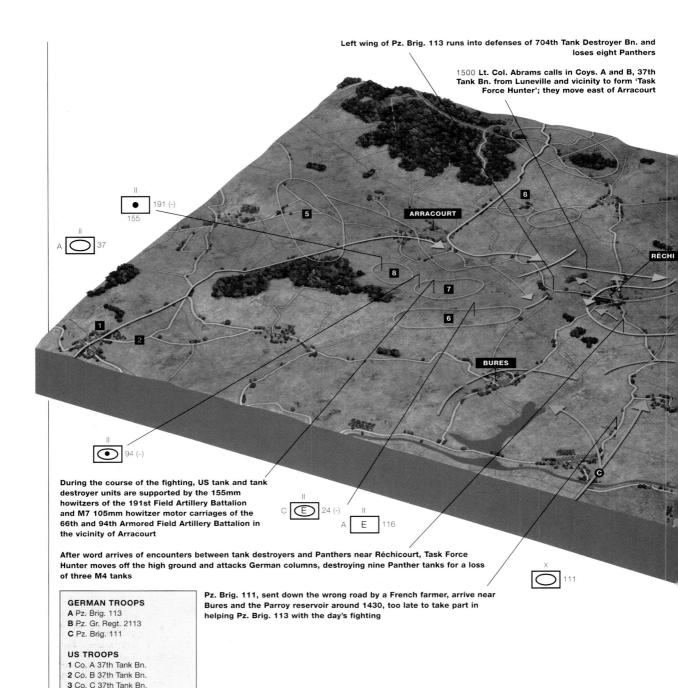

Left wing of Pz. Brig. 113 runs into defenses of 704th Tank Destroyer Bn. and loses eight Panthers

1500 **Lt. Col. Abrams calls in Coys. A and B, 37th Tank Bn. from Luneville and vicinity to form 'Task Force Hunter'; they move east of Arracourt**

II
● 191 (-)
155

A ⬭ II 37

ARRACOURT

5

8

RÉCHI

8

7

6

2

1

BURES

94 (-)

During the course of the fighting, US tank and tank destroyer units are supported by the 155mm howitzers of the 191st Field Artillery Battalion and M7 105mm howitzer motor carriages of the 66th and 94th Armored Field Artillery Battalion in the vicinity of Arracourt

C Ⓔ 24 (-)
A E 116

After word arrives of encounters between tank destroyers and Panthers near Réchicourt, Task Force Hunter moves off the high ground and attacks German columns, destroying nine Panther tanks for a loss of three M4 tanks

C

X
⬭ 111

Pz. Brig. 111, sent down the wrong road by a French farmer, arrive near Bures and the Parroy reservoir around 1430, too late to take part in helping Pz. Brig. 113 with the day's fighting

GERMAN TROOPS
A Pz. Brig. 113
B Pz. Gr. Regt. 2113
C Pz. Brig. 111

US TROOPS
1 Co. A 37th Tank Bn.
2 Co. B 37th Tank Bn.
3 Co. C 37th Tank Bn.
4 Co. D 37th Tank Bn.
5 704th Tank Destroyer Bn.
6 66th Armd. Field Arty. Bn.
7 94th Armd. Field Arty. Bn.
8 191st Armd. Field Arty. Bn.

TANK BATTLE AT ARRACOURT, 19 SEPTEMBER 1944

Under pressure from Berlin, Manteuffel sent Pz. Brig. 113 to destroy the dispositions of the US 4th Armd. Corps around Arracourt.

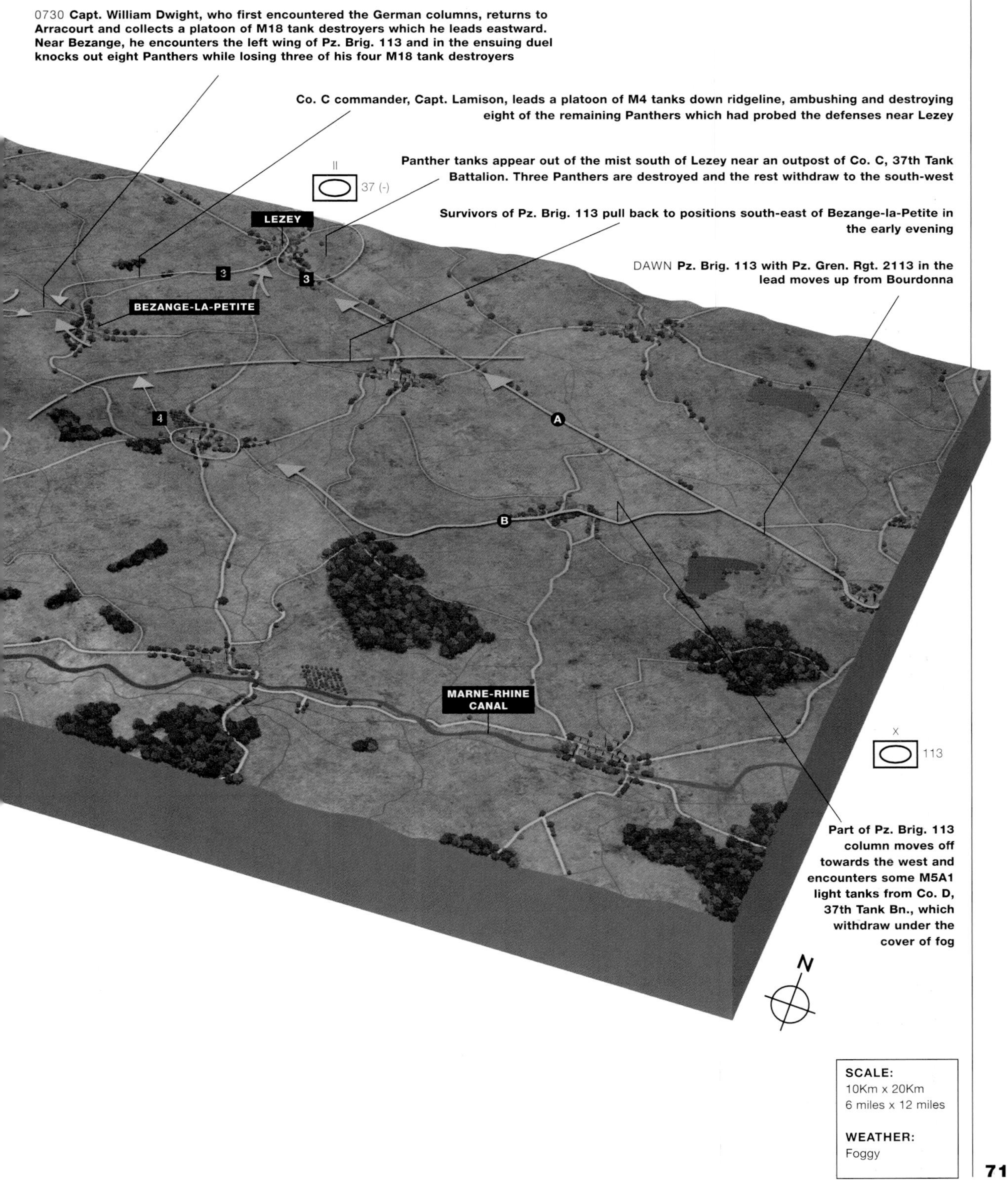

0730 **Capt. William Dwight**, who first encountered the German columns, returns to Arracourt and collects a platoon of M18 tank destroyers which he leads eastward. Near Bezange, he encounters the left wing of Pz. Brig. 113 and in the ensuing duel knocks out eight Panthers while losing three of his four M18 tank destroyers

Co. C commander, **Capt. Lamison**, leads a platoon of M4 tanks down ridgeline, ambushing and destroying eight of the remaining Panthers which had probed the defenses near Lezey

Panther tanks appear out of the mist south of Lezey near an outpost of Co. C, 37th Tank Battalion. Three Panthers are destroyed and the rest withdraw to the south-west

Survivors of Pz. Brig. 113 pull back to positions south-east of Bezange-la-Petite in the early evening

DAWN **Pz. Brig. 113** with **Pz. Gren. Rgt. 2113** in the lead moves up from Bourdonna

II 37 (-)

LEZEY

3

3

BEZANGE-LA-PETITE

4

A

B

MARNE-RHINE CANAL

X 113

Part of Pz. Brig. 113 column moves off towards the west and encounters some M5A1 light tanks from Co. D, 37th Tank Bn., which withdraw under the cover of fog

N

SCALE:
10Km x 20Km
6 miles x 12 miles

WEATHER:
Foggy

71

Lezey. On the way to Lezey, near Bezange-la-Petite, the platoon encountered the lead elements of the western spearhead of Pz. Brig. 113. Unnoticed in the thick fog, the M18s deployed in a shallow depression and began engaging the German tanks at a range of only 150 yards from hull-down positions. In the sharp firefight that ensued, seven German tanks were knocked out, but three of the four M18 Hellcats were put out of action as well. The German column retreated.

Pz. Brig. 113 continued its attack towards Réchicourt-la-Petite. Another platoon of M18 Hellcats of the 704th Tank Destroyer Battalion struck at one of the German columns, knocking out eight Panthers and causing the attack to falter. By mid-afternoon, the tank destroyers had knocked out 19 tanks but had suffered significant casualties, including the battalion commander, who was killed by mortar fire.

As the tank fighting intensified, Abrams radioed his scattered tank companies, ordering them to rally near Arracourt. In the early afternoon, Cos. A and B were united under Task Force Hunter and sent to counter-attack near Réchicourt. The ensuing tank battle led to the destruction of nine more Panther tanks, at a cost of three M4 medium tanks.

Patton visited Arracourt late that day and talked with Gen. Wood, the divisional commander. Wood indicated that his units had destroyed 43 enemy tanks during the fighting, mostly factory-fresh Panthers, at a cost of six killed and three wounded, plus three M18 tank destroyers and five M4 tanks knocked out. Patton believed that the German strength in the area had been spent, and he ordered Wood to continue the advance on Saareguemines the next day.

The opportunity to hit the 4th Armd. Div. with a concentrated blow by two panzer brigades was foiled by poor map-reading. Pz. Brig. 111 did not reach the Arracourt area until the middle of the afternoon, and played no role in the day's fighting. The 58th Panzer Corps commander estimated that his units had lost 50 tanks destroyed or damaged during the day's fighting. Blaskowitz was furious at the failure of the 58th Panzer Corps and ordered Manteuffel to continue the attack the next day regardless of the casualties.

In the early morning of 20 September, CCA of 4th Armd. Div. moved out from the area near Lezey on their planned offensive. They had reached Dieuze when the division's rear elements near Arracourt reported that the German tanks were attacking again from the Parroy woods towards the town. This time, it was the tanks of Pz. Brig. 111 which had missed the previous day's battle. About eight German tanks had appeared out of the mist about 1,000 yards from the 191st Field Artillery Battalion as it was preparing to limber up and move out. The 155mm howitzers were quickly swung around and began to take the tanks under fire at point-blank range. A small number of tanks and tank destroyers from other units showed up, and the panzer attack was beaten off under intense fire.

Col. Abrams ordered the 37th Tank Bn. back towards Lezey to clear the area of German tanks once and for all. In the meantime, Capt. Junghannis's PzKpfw IV company, supported by anti-tank guns, took up ambush positions on the approaches to the area where the earlier fighting had taken place. When Co. C, 37th Tank Bn. crested the rise, they were hit with a volley from the tanks and anti-tank guns below, losing a half-dozen M4 tanks in a few seconds. The Americans pulled back over the rise and waited for Co. B to reach them. After forming up, the two companies maneuvered to gain a better position and in the ensuing tank fighting, knocked out 11 German tanks while losing

A medic from the 37th Tank Bn. tends to a wounded tank crew while the fighting rages in the field above, near Arracourt on 24 September 1944. Several tanks are silhouetted against the skyline. (US Army)

another six themselves. A further five Panthers were knocked out later in the afternoon when the American task force reached Bures.

While CCA, 4th Armd. Div. was fighting with the panzers for most of 20 September, CCB was attacking near Chateau Salins, threatening to drive a wedge between Manteuffel's Fifth Panzer Army and the First Army to the north.

Blaskowitz was becoming increasingly frustrated by Manteuffel's failures and accused him of limiting his units to defensive action. Pz. Brig. 113 had remained largely inactive during the fighting on 20 September, and Pz. Brig. 111 had managed to put only a couple of companies of tanks into action during the whole day, having bungled their part in the previous day's attack. Manteuffel, in turn, complained about the poor combat value of the panzer brigades, but he was lectured by Blaskowitz on tactics. When American tanks pushed German troops out of Moncourt later in the evening, Manteuffel used it as an excuse to request a general withdrawal of the 57th Panzer Corps east of the Parroy woods. Outraged, Blaskowitz ordered him to counterattack again the next day.

TANK DUEL: Panthers emerge from the early morning mist near Arracourt and are taken under fire at close range by M4 medium tanks of Co. C, 37th Tank Bn., 4th Armd. Div.

TonyBryan. 03/00

Hitler was furious to learn that the carefully husbanded panzer brigades had been squandered with so little effect and that his plans for an early and quick victory over Patton had been frustrated. On 21 September, he sacked Blaskowitz and replaced him with General Hermann Balck, who that same day ordered a shift in plans. The focus was now coming north of Arracourt, from around Chateau Salins. A combined operation by First Army and Fifth Panzer Army would aim at seizing the key road junction at Moyenvic. This confused the effort even more, since most of the German armor was south of Arracourt. As a result, there was little fighting on 21 September while the Germans shuffled their command.

The German attack on the morning of 22 September got off to a late start due to the tardy arrival of an infantry battalion. The northern flank of CCA, 4th Armd. Div. was screened by elements of 25th Cav. Sqn. In the thick morning fog, the German columns managed to get close to the cavalry outposts before being observed. A series of skirmishes broke out, in which seven M5A1 light tanks of Co. F were knocked out while desperately trying to fend off attacks by the much more powerful German tanks. The German attack was blunted when it ran into a thin

screen of M18 Hellcat tank destroyers of Co. C, 704th Tank Destroyer Battalion. This knocked out three German tanks. The late start of the attack meant that the fog was starting to lift, and this made the German columns vulnerable to air attack. For the first time in several days, the P-47 Thunderbolts of the XIX TAC came roaring over the battlefield, strafing and bombing the German columns.

While the cavalry screen delayed the German attack, Abrams reoriented the 37th Tank Bn. northward and occupied a hill near Trois Crois which looked down into the valley east of Juvelize, where the German reinforcements were moving forward. Co. A, 37th Tank Bn. took the German tanks under fire at ranges of 400 to 2,000 yards as well as calling in field artillery fire on them. During the fighting, the Pz. Brig. 111 commander, Col. Heinrich von Bronsart-Schellendorf, was killed by machine-gun fire. Some of his officers felt that he had given up hope after another tongue lashing earlier in the morning from Manteuffel, and had carelessly exposed himself to hostile fire.

The retreating German columns were pounded by artillery fire from M7 105mm HMCs and by the continued attacks of P-47 Thunderbolts. After the Luftwaffe refused his pleas for air support, Manteuffel committed his last armored reserve – the surviving tanks from Pz. Brig. 113. This had no perceptible effect. By the end of the day, Pz. Brig. 111 was down to seven tanks and 80 men from an original strength of over 90 tanks and 2,500 troops. The following day, the Pz. Brig. 113 commander, Col. Erich von Seckendorf, was killed when his half-track command vehicle was strafed by a P-47 from the 405th Group.

In the three days of fighting from 19 to 22 September, the 4th Armd. Div.'s Combat Command A had lost 14 M4 medium and seven M5A1 light tanks as well as 25 men killed and 88 wounded. In return they had effectively shattered two panzer brigades.

Any thoughts of reinforcing the Fifth Panzer Army with more armor were rejected by Hitler due to the significant shifts in the strategic situation in late September. The Lorraine panzer offensive had been planned in early September, when Hitler had thought that Patton's thrust would be the first to reach German soil. By late September, it was becoming obvious that the Allies had other plans. On 17 September, two days before the Lorraine panzer attacks had started in earnest, the Allies had staged Operation Market-Garden, a massive airborne operation in the Netherlands combined with a tank thrust by the British 21st Army Group aimed at seizing the Arnhem River to strike into the Rhine from the north. This was supported by an intensified attack by Hodges' First Army in Belgium. Furthermore, on 15 September, the US 3rd Armd. Div. had punched a hole through the Westwall, threatening the German city of Aachen. By 24 September, after the first series of Lorraine tank battles had ended, Rundstedt was pleading with Hitler to shift the surviving armor northward to prevent an American entry into Aachen. Although Hitler would not provide any more reinforcements, neither would he abandon his plans in Lorraine. The belated arrival of the 11th Pz. Div. marked a new stage in the Lorraine tank fighting.

Bradley contacted Patton on 23 September and informed him that due to a lack of supplies, the Third Army would have to take up defensive positions. The 6th Armd. Div. was being taken away from him, so the armored forces needed for a drive on the Rhine would not be available. Furthermore, Haislip's XV Corps would be shifted to the 6th Army Group at the end of the month, removing a second armored division and leaving Patton with only two. The next day, Patton met with his three corps commanders, Walker, Eddy, and Haislip, and they agreed on a line that could be defended by the remaining forces.

The German attacks resumed on 24 September. Based on Balck's new plan, the focus shifted to the formations of the German First Army, mainly the 559th Volksgrenadier Division supported by remaining tanks of Pz. Brig. 106. The CCB of 4th Armd. Div. was holding a screening position in front of the 35th Inf. Div. near Chateau Salins when the Germans began the attack with a heavy concentration of artillery around 0830. Two regiments of infantry attacked the CCB positions, combined with a tank attack on the right flank. The 80 percent cloud cover made flying inadvisable, but two squadrons of P-47s were vectored into the area using radar. Around 1000, the P-47s found a gap in the clouds and made a skip-bombing attack on the Panthers from an altitude of about 15 feet, then returned to strafe. Within 15 minutes, the German attack had collapsed and they withdrew, leaving behind about 300 dead and 11 tanks. Patton recommended the Medal of Honor for the pilot who led the attack.

As Balck quickly realized, First Army did not have the resources to attack the American positions. Once again the focus shifted to Fifth Panzer Army. By the following day, Manteuffel had managed to scrape together about 50 tanks, including 16 from the newly arrived 11th Pz. Div. By this stage, the panzer brigades had been decimated and were no longer fit for operations. Manteuffel received permission to merge their tanks and troops with the divisions which could utilize their remaining resources. Pz. Brig. 111 went to the 11 Pz. Div.; Pz. Brig. 112 to 21 Pz. Div.; and Pz. Brig. 113 to 15 Pz. Gren. Div. Manteuffel did not want a repeat of the 22 September fighting and had troops scout the US lines in advance of the attack. Reconnaissance indicated that the crossroads town of Moyenvic was unoccupied on the evening of 24 September, so this became the initial objective of the attack. A quick and largely uncontested advance in the morning convinced Manteuffel to continue the offensive, and attacks were launched all along the salient held by CCA, 4th Armd. Div. The attacks were all beaten back, as the Americans held the high ground and had an advantage in both tanks and artillery.

As a result of the 24 September decision to shift Third Army over to the defensive, on 25 September, the CCA was ordered to withdraw about two miles from its exposed positions around Juvelize, back towards Arracourt to create a more defensible line. The CCA commander, Col. Bruce Clarke, selected the Arracourt region as the hills around the town gave his unit a good vantage point, looking down on German positions in the neighboring area. The withdrawal was also marked by a shift in the composition of the forces. Abrams' 37th Tank Bn. was pulled back to rest and refit, and the line was now held by three of 4th Armd. Div.'s armored infantry battalions. Realignment was completed on 26 September, and the German attacks would now be faced by dismounted armored infantry dug in along the crest of the hills to the south and east of Arracourt.

Manteuffel used the uncontested withdrawal by Clarke's CCA to claim a local victory, and Fifth Panzer Army occupied Juvelize and Coincourt.

On 27 September, the German attacks resumed. By this time, the armored forces in the sector consisted of 24 Panthers, six PzKpfw IVs, and some assault guns. Manteuffel sought to secure two hills on the southern

JABO STRIKE: An aerial view of P-47 D-25 Thunderbolts of the 405th Fighter Group, XIX TAC as they go out on a tank-hunting mission over Lorraine.

CHOW
HOUND

2Ng

416197

228445

420535

G9   6

G9   B

G9   W

Tony Bryan. 03/00

flank of the 4th Armd. Div. positions which overlooked the Fifth Panzer Army positions. The aim of the attack was to seize the camel-back plateau of Hills 318 and 293. He ordered Gen. Wietersheim to concentrate a battlegroup in an attack from Bures towards Arracourt. Kampfgruppe Hammon consisted of the remnants of Pz. Brig. 113 and the division's reconnaissance battalion with about 25 tanks. From his experience on the Western Front, Wietersheim was opposed to concentrating all the armor, feeling that it would be too vulnerable to air and artillery attack; based on his Eastern Front experience, Manteuffel was equally adamant that the armor be concentrated and not committed piecemeal.

The assault started with a diversionary advance by the rest of the division on the eastern end of the salient which seized Lezey and Ley, while Pz. Gren. Rgt. 111 supported by a few tanks occupied the village of Bezange-la-Petite below the positions of the 10th Armd. Inf. Bn. on Hill 265. The German infantry clawed their way to the top of Hill 265, but in bitter fighting were finally pushed off the hill. Lt. James Field received the Medal of Honor for gallantry in the clash. The position on Hill 265 was reinforced by a platoon of tank destroyers and a platoon of engineers, and another German attack at 2150 that night was successfully pushed back. On the north-east flank, Pz. Gren. Rgt. 110 moved into Xanrey, but while regrouping around 1600, it was hit by a counterattack by M4 tanks of the 35th Tank Bn., losing 135 grenadiers and being forced to retreat.

The main attack by the German battlegroup began around 1000 but moved only 1,800 yards when brought under intense fire from six field artillery battalions supporting Clarke's CCA. The German attack was halted and the panzers withdrew. Gen. Wietersheim shifted the 2nd battalion of 110th Pz. Gren. Rgt. to support the southern sector, and the next day the attack resumed. The panzer grenadiers infiltrated past the farm at the base of Hill 318, and after bitter fighting, Kampfgruppe Hammon reached the top of the hill and the edge of the neighboring woods. The crest of Hill 318 became the focus of the fighting over the next few days.

The crew of a PzKpfw IV command tank, the company commander in the center, from Pz Abt 2111 of Pz. Brig. 111 shortly before the tank fighting around Arracourt in late September. The tank has the armor skirts around the turret and the command radio antenna is evident over the shoulder of the second tanker from the left. The captain is decorated with the Iron Cross First and Second Class and also wears the insignia for those who served in the Crimea campaign on the Eastern Front in 1942. (USNA)

The panzer grenadiers of Pz. Brig. 111 check their weapons prior to another attack on Arracourt in late September 1944 while French townspeople look on. (USNA)

Manteuffel's orders for the next day were blunt: "Take Hills 293 and 318, then press farther toward the north-west in the direction of Arracourt." At dawn on 28 September, the 51st Armd. Inf. Bn. retook the forward slope of Hill 318, but the fighting surged across the crest during the day. There were 107 fighter-bomber sorties in the fighting, with the P-47s leveling the village of Bures and badly disrupting the German reinforcements concentrated there. After pushing back three more German attacks, the GIs retook Hill 318 around noon. The German grenadiers had received little artillery support, since the batteries had moved to new positions during the night and their forward observers were not in place until later in the day.

A GI inspects one of the StuG III assault guns knocked out during the fighting around Luneville. The side Schurzen, or armor shields, dubbed "bazooka pants" by the GIs, are missing, but their attachment rails are evident. Although widely believed to be a form of protection against bazookas, PIATs, and other shaped-charge anti-tank weapons, they were in fact used as protection against Soviet anti-tank rifles, and so were often removed on the Western Front, where they had no defensive value. Indeed, they would enhance the penetration of a bazooka warhead by optimizing the stand-off distance to the main armor. (US Army)

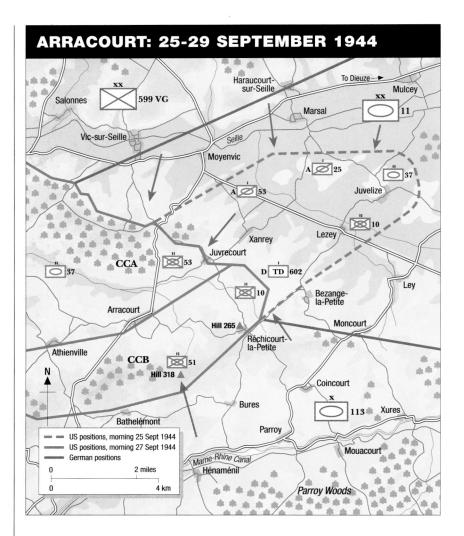

ARRACOURT: 25-29 SEPTEMBER 1944

A final German daylight attack was broken up by American artillery fire before it could reach its objective. After dark, the Germans sent in another assault force, supported by tanks, which secured the south face of the hill. The 51st Armored Infantry withdrew to the north slope, but were hit by a heavy German artillery barrage. The 4th Armd. Div. responded by a four artillery battalion fire-strike on the south slope, followed by a 51st Armored Infantry counterattack which secured the southern high ground around midnight.

The fighting on neighboring Hill 265 was nearly as intense. At 1900, a German infantry attack against Co. A, 10th Armd. Inf. Bn. forced one of its platoons to pull back, but the attackers were brought under intense American artillery fire. Wietersheim requested to Manteuffel that his troops be allowed to break off the attacks to get some rest or they would simply lose their combat effectiveness. Manteuffel refused and, under extreme pressure from Berlin, he insisted that the attacks continue.

By dawn of 29 September, the 11th Pz. Div. had reinforced its units opposite Hills 265 and 318 from other sectors. Massing near the smoldering ruins of Bures, its forces included the reconnaissance regiment of the 11th Pz. Div., a battalion from Pz. Gren. Rgt. 110, an

A German StuG III assault gun lies in ruins, its engine deck blown off, in the outskirts of Luneville on 27 September 1944. The StuG III was used primarily to provide direct fire support for German infantry formations, but its 75mm gun was also effective against Allied tanks. This is probably one of the StuG IIIs from Pz. Brig. 111 lost in the fighting there. (US Army)

armored engineer company, and the remaining armor of Panzer Brigades 111 and 113. The armored strength in the sector included 18 PzKpfw IVs, 20 Panthers, and 11 Flakpanzer IVs. Another attack on Hill 318 pushed the 51st Armd. Inf. Bn. back about 500 yards, and the Germans had reoccupied the forward crest of the hill by 1015.

Given the heavy casualties suffered by the 51st Armd. Inf. Bn., Col. Clarke ordered forward a company of M4 medium tanks from the 8th Tank Bn. They reached the beleaguered infantry during the morning, and in the course of the day's fighting were credited with knocking out eight more panzers. As the morning fog lifted, a tactical air liaison officer with the group directed P-47 Thunderbolt strikes on the panzers in the field below Hill 318, where they were massing for another attack. Without the fog for protection, the troops were exposed. The initial air attacks were ineffective, as the fighter-bombers were diverted from a planned mission over Metz armed only with propaganda leaflets. However, during the course of the day, the 405th Fighter Group carried out several low-altitude air strikes against the German forces preparing to assault the hill. Besides knocking out tanks with bombs and rocket fire, the air strikes managed to drive a number of German tanks out of the cover of woods, where they were then struck by artillery fire.

By the middle of the afternoon, the German troops were in full retreat. After three days of intense fighting, with little sleep and heavy casualties, many of the German units had disintegrated, and the commander of Kampfgruppe Bode suffered a nervous breakdown. The German staging area at the base of the plateau had the Marne Canal at its back, and many of the troops feared that the Americans might charge down off the plateau and trap them against the water. The 15th Pz. Gren. Div. was forced to set up a straggler line with tanks near Parroy in an attempt to restore some order. The surviving Flakpanzers were positioned in Parroy and Bures in an attempt to ward off the continuing air attacks, but they were almost completely ineffective. The corps commander's report to Manteuffel was blunt: "Hill triangle lost. Troops exhausted, need rest." A total of 23 tanks and several armored half-tracks had been knocked out, according to German accounts of the fighting. Only four tanks remained operational by the end of the day, though

The crew of an M4 medium tank, commanded by Sgt. Timothy Dunn of the 37th Tank Bn., bed down for the night in a field to the north-east of Arracourt on the evening of 26 September 1944. The crewman at the front of the tank is removing the Culin device, a set of steel prongs designed to cut through the thick hedgerows found in Normandy.

stragglers continued to filter back to German lines over the next day. Tanks that had been abandoned were attacked and burned out by P-47 fighter-bombers.

The fighting on neighboring Hill 265 was mainly directed against the right flank held by Co. A, 10th Armd. Inf. Bn. The GIs were finally pushed back to the reverse slope of the hill, but held their positions at nightfall. Exhausted, the German infantry withdrew into the town of Bezange below. Some German units remained trapped on the hills between Hills 265 and 318 but escaped under the cover of darkness when it became apparent that the other battlegroups were withdrawing.

The attack on 29 September represented the last major attempt by Fifth Panzer Army to cut off the Third Army's spearhead near Arracourt. The last four days of attacks on CCA, 4th Armd. Div. had already cost the Fifth Panzer Army about 700 killed and 300 wounded, as well as 14 PzKpfw IVs and 22 Panther tanks. Of the 262 tanks and assault guns deployed by the German units in the week of fighting near Arracourt, 86 were destroyed and only 62 were operational at the end of the month. The 4th Armd. Div., which had borne the brunt of the Arracourt tank fighting, lost 41 M4 medium tanks and seven M5A1 light tanks during the whole month of September. Casualties were 225 killed and 648 wounded.

On 29 September, while the fighting was still raging on the hills south of Arracourt, the new Army Group G commander, Gen. Balck, visited the Western Front commander, von Rundstedt at his HQ in Bad Kreuznach. Balck told the field marshal that if his forces did not receive reinforcements with at least 140 tanks and more artillery, it would be impossible to continue any offensive actions. Von Rundstedt replied that reinforcements were out of the question, and he tacitly accepted that the Lorraine panzer offensive would come to an end without fulfilling Hitler's objective. At 2300 hours, Balck told Manteuffel to call off the attack. The battered 11th Pz. Div. would be pulled out of the line and defensive positions secured. Hitler, preoccupied with the airborne assault at Arnhem and the penetrations of the Westwall near Aachen, ignored yet another defeat of his preposterous schemes.

STALEMATE

By the end of September, the Lorraine fighting had ended in stalemate. Deprived of units and supplies, Patton's Third Army was in no position to plan further offensives. Yet September had seen real accomplishments. Patton's aggressive actions during the month, in spite of frequent supply shortfalls, had pushed his Third Army over the formidable barrier of the Moselle. Under a less aggressive commander, the Third Army would not have crossed the river and would have faced the daunting task of making the crossing in winter against a more firmly established German line. The Lorraine operations in September 1944 placed the Third Army in a firm position for later operations against the Saar and was instrumental in Patton's ability to conduct the rescue of Bastogne two months later, during the Ardennes fighting.

The controversies surrounding Eisenhower, Bradley, and Montgomery over strategic issues have obscured the role played by the Third Army in the broader context of Allied operations in September. In Normandy, the British forces had acted as a magnet, attracting German panzer forces and allowing the US offensive at St. Lo. In September, Patton's aggressive actions in Lorraine attracted the bulk of the panzer forces, permitting the British forces to conduct their bold Market-Garden offensive relatively unhindered by tank attack. Without Patton's actions in Lorraine, Market-Garden would have had even less chance of success and other Allied actions in Belgium would have faced stiffer resistance.

Patton's ambitions to push his forces beyond the Westwall and into the Saar in September proved impossible. This was not due to any

A tanker of the HQ company of 37th Tank Bn., Private Kenneth Boyer, on board his M4 (105mm) assault gun on 26 September 1944 during the Arracourt fighting. The M4 105mm assault gun resembled the normal M4 tank, but instead of a 75mm gun, it had a 105mm howitzer. These assault guns were attached to the head-quarters companies of tank battalions to provide direct and indirect fire support.

Capt. J. F. Brady, commander of Co. A, 35th Tank Bn., was decorated with the Silver Star for his actions during the fighting around Arracourt. He is wearing the standard US Army tanker's helmet, derived from football helmets, and is seen using the tank's intercom microphone. (US Army)

tactical failure: the strategic planning of SHAEF placed greater emphasis on operations north of the Ardennes and allotted vital supplies accordingly. The Metz fortress prevented the advance of XX Corps, and the attacks by Fifth Panzer Army in late September derailed a narrow thrust by XII Corps. It is quite possible that Patton would have been able to push beyond the Westwall had the Fifth Panzer Army counterattacks not taken place or had he been allotted additional forces and supplies. The chief of staff of Army Group G, Col. Frederich von Mellenthin, later argued that Patton could have penetrated into Germany in mid-September if he had had the resources, since German reserves in the area were so weak. Distracted by the debates over the broad versus narrow front, and the resulting compromise decision to stage Operation Market-Garden, Eisenhower opted for the safe course in Lorraine and instructed Patton to cool his heels on the eastern bank of the Moselle. An opportunity in Lorraine and the Saar was given up for a riskier but potentially more lucrative gamble in Holland.

Total Third Army armored vehicle losses in September included 49 light tanks and 151 medium tanks and tank destroyers. A total of 392 tanks were issued in September, so by the end of the month, Third Army had more than replaced all of its losses.

From a German perspective, the Lorraine fighting had mixed results. Fifth Panzer Army had been shattered and was incapable of any further attacks. Hitler's plans to cut off Patton's forces were grossly unrealistic given the disparity in forces in the region. While offensives by German panzer forces at near parity strength to their adversary may have been successful on the Eastern Front, they were not possible against the US Army in 1944. Both German panzer counteroffensives in the late summer of 1944 had failed – the August attack by the 47th Panzer Corps and the 1st SS Panzer Corps at Mortain, and the September operation by

One of the heaviest field artillery weapons in US Army service during the war was the M1 240mm howitzer. It could fire a 360lb high explosive round to a range of about five miles. This weapon from the 278th Field Artillery Battalion is in support of Third Army operations in Lorraine on 29 September 1944. (US Army)

the Fifth Panzer Army near Arracourt. In both cases, the German forces had enjoyed advantages in armored vehicle strength in the attacking sector but had been unable to exploit these advantages due to US superiority in firepower and the declining offensive skills of the German forces. Even someone as deluded as Hitler drew the appropriate lessons from these two failed counteroffensives. Mortain and Arracourt were to Hitler's later Ardennes offensive as Dieppe was to the Allied Normandy offensive: a clear reminder that half-hearted operations against a skilled opponent had no chance of success. In late September, with the prospects for success in Lorraine evaporating, Hitler began plans for Operation Wacht-am-Rhein, the Ardennes counteroffensive. No longer underestimating the US Army, he planned a breakthrough operation by 26 German divisions against four American divisions.

Although the panzer counteroffensive against Patton had failed, this can obscure the more important consequence of German operations. In late August 1944, Allied leaders had believed that Germany was on the brink of collapse. By late September 1944, they were not so optimistic. After the catastrophic defeats in the summer of 1944, the Wehrmacht had recovered and re-established a firm defensive position along the western German frontier. The September recovery is appropriately called "the miracle in the west" in German histories. Commanders like Blaskowitz seldom attract attention in the same way as the more flamboyant leaders such as Model and Manteuffel, but his skilled and patient efforts were instrumental in re-establishing a firm German defensive line in front of the Westwall. While these actions reaffirmed the reputation of the Wehrmacht for its tenacity in adversity, the strategic

The US Army continued to locate disabled and abandoned equipment from the Arracourt fighting for weeks afterwards. Here, a GI is seen in the commander's cupola of a PzKpfw IV medium tank near Grandvillars on 18 October 1944. The turret is traversed to the rear to discourage US troops from firing on it. (US Army)

consequences for Germany were tragic, ensuring a further seven months of war and millions of additional civilian casualties, mostly in Germany itself.

Of the 616 tanks and assault guns committed to the Lorraine fighting in September, there were only 127 still operational by 1 October. Losses had amounted to 101 PzKpfw IVs, 118 Panthers, and 221 assault guns and tank destroyers. A further 148 armored vehicles were on hand but were damaged and in need of repair. German losses in men and equipment in Lorraine were far higher than those of the Americans – and far more difficult to replace.

The popular myth of the superiority of German tanks in combat in north-west Europe is belied by the record of their actual performance. In an engagement of the type seen around Arracourt, with both sides in an offensive posture and neither side enjoying particular numerical advantage, panzer units were overcome by superior American training and tactics. While airpower played an important role in some encounters, such as Dompaire, most of the fighting took place under rainy and foggy conditions where airpower could not intervene to a significant extent. German tanks and anti-tank guns could still exact a painful toll against American tanks when skillfully employed from defensive positions, as would be evident in the remaining months of the war. However, the same was true of American tank and tank destroyer units, as was seen in the difficult opening weeks of the Ardennes offensive, when the panzer offensive was stopped in its tracks far short of its objectives. Unlike the Eastern Front, there were very few meeting engagements or offensive panzer operations in north-west Europe in 1944-45, so perceptions of the relative merits of German and Allied armoured unit performance is skewed by the natural advantages enjoyed by a force fighting almost exclusively on the defensive. The German tank units of 1944-45 were only an emaciated reflection of their glory days in 1939-43.

THE BATTLEFIELD TODAY

L ike most World War II battlefields, there are few signs of the conflict in Lorraine in 1944. Lorraine may be a traditional warpath between Germany and France, but it is also a natural trade route which has prospered in the half-century since World War II. Its rivers, roads, and canals, and its proximity to French and German industrial regions have made it a natural business center. Traces of war disappear quickly from the countryside, but the farmlands where the battles were fought are certainly closer to their wartime appearance than the towns and cities.

There are no major museums to the Lorraine campaign in the area. This is not surprising, given the relative scale of military events in the region over the past several centuries, such as at neighboring Verdun. Indeed, World War I memorials outnumber World War II memorials by a large measure, and it is hard to find a town without a remembrance of the valiant poilus of 1914-18. However, many of the towns in the area have small memorials to the September fighting. For example, in the hamlet of Mairy, there is a street named Rue de 8 Septembre 1944 after the fighting there between Pz. Brig. 106 and the 90th Infantry Division, and most towns have small plaques identifying historical sites.

The most extensive memorial is to Gen. Jacques Leclerc and the French 2nd Armored Division. It is located appropriately enough between the towns of Dompaire and Lamerey. There is an M4A1 on display at the site in the markings of *Corse*, the command tank of Adjutant-Chef Titeux of the 3rd Platoon, 2nd Squadron of the 12e Régiment des Chasseurs d'Afrique. However, the tank named *Corse* that fought at Dompaire was an M4A2 serial number 420050 and the M4A1 tank on display may have been the one that replaced it in 1945.

Not surprisingly, tanks have proven to be one of the most popular forms of memorial to the fighting in Lorraine. In the town of Arracourt, opposite a World War I memorial, is an M4A4 medium tank in the markings of Co. A, 37th Tank Bn., 4th Armd. Div. This tank has battle damage on the left side, but is an ex-French Army vehicle, since the US Army seldom used the M4A4 in combat and 4th Armd. Div. at the time was equipped with the M4 version of this tank series. Another M4 is preserved in Ville-sur-Illon to commemorate the fighting by the GTL Langlade HQ. There is an M4A1 (76mm) in US Army markings on display in the Place Stanislas at Laxou outside Nancy, but it is not clear whether this tank was an actual veteran of the fighting or an ex-French Army tank. An M8 75mm HMC in French 2nd Armored Division markings is preserved at Andelot as a memorial to the fighting on 11/12 September 1944, and an M4A1 medium tank is preserved at Dijon to celebrate the link-up between Patton's Third Army and Devers' 6th Army Group.

Remarkably enough, at least four more armored vehicles have survived from the Lorraine fighting, though they are located elsewhere. Two of the

Panther tanks that were recovered by the French 2nd Armored Division in Dompaire were sent back to Paris in 1944 to celebrate the victory. For many years, they sat outside the gates of the Invalides military museum in central Paris, emblazoned with the division's Cross-of-Lorraine insignia on their glacis plate. About a decade ago, they were removed to the tank museum at the French Army cavalry school at Saumur. The hull of a third Panther was fished out of the Parroy lake, where it had become trapped in 1944, and this too ended up in Saumur. Finally, an M10 tank destroyer of the RBFM which fought at Dompaire, named *Siroco*, was also preserved and is currently on display in Saumur. Commanded by Second-maitre Krokenberger and serving with the 3rd Platoon, 4th Squadron of the RBSM, *Sirocco* was credited with knocking out three Panther tanks during the fighting at Dompaire as part of Group Massu.

Memorials to the Lorraine fighting have also taken other forms. Two of today's most modern main battle tanks are named after tank commanders who first made their reputations in the Lorraine campaign. The US Army's current tank, the M1 Abrams, was developed in the 1970s when Creighton Abrams was the army chief-of-staff. After having personally experienced the struggle of the US Army's inadequate M4 medium tank against the German Panther at Arracourt, Abrams was determined that the new M1 tank would be superior to any it opposed. Following his death in 1974, the M1 tank was named in his honor. France followed a similar tradition, when its new main battle tank entered service in the early 1980s, naming it the Leclerc, after the commander of the French 2nd Armored Division.

A GUIDE TO FURTHER READING

This book was prepared largely through the use of superb library and archival records of the Military History Institute (MHI) of the US Army War College at Carlisle Barracks, Pennsylvania. Besides its extensive collection of records and unit histories of the US Army in Lorraine in 1944, the MHI is also the repository for a large collection of interviews with senior German commanders collected after the war by US Army historians. These include several hundred pages of interviews about the Lorraine fighting with many of the major German figures, including Manteuffel, his aide, and many other army, corps, and division commanders.

To list all the books, articles, and documents used in the preparation of this book would take many pages. Instead, the focus here is on the essential and more readily available accounts.

Omar Bradley, *A Soldier's Story* (Henry Holt, 1951). Bradley's memoirs are more detailed than Patton's on many of the controversies, and this book has been reprinted in several different editions.

H. M. Cole, *The Lorraine Campaign* (US Army, 1981). This is the official US Army account of the Lorraine campaign by the Third Army's historian and remains the best and single most essential volume on the subject. It is still in print by the US Government Printing Office.

David Eisenhower, *Eisenhower at War 1943-1945* (Random House, 1986). One of the best accounts of the 1944 Eisenhower-Montgomery controversy from Ike's perspective, written by one of his grandsons.

Carlo D'Este, *Patton: A Genius for War* (HarperCollins, 1995). An assessment of Patton by one of the younger generation of American military historians.

Ian Gooderson, *Air Power at the Battlefront: Allied Close-air Support in Europe 1943-45* (Frank Cass, 1998). An intriguing new look at the effectiveness of close-air support.

Thomas Jentz, *Panzertruppen*, Vol 2 (Schiffer, 1996). A detailed look at the organization, unit strength, tactics and other aspects of the panzer force, based on archival records.

Ronald McNair, 1944: *Les Panzers en Lorraine* (Heimdal, 1984). This is a bound edition of articles appearing in the French historical journal 39-45. It is one of the best treatments of the Arracourt tank battles from the German perspective. A shorter English treatment is available in the British journal After the Battle, No 83.

Jacques Salbaing, *La Victoire de Leclerc à Dompaire* (Muller, 1997). This short French book provides a detailed examination of the destruction of Pz. Brig. 112 at Dompaire by the French 2nd Armored Division.

George S. Patton Jr, *War As I Knew It* (Houghton-Mifflin, 1947). Patton's personal account of his role in World War II; available in many different editions.

Russell Weigley, *Eisenhower's Lieutenants: The Campaigns of France and Germany 1944-45* (Indiana Univ Press, 1981). A critical assessment of the performance of the US Army in north-west Europe, and still one of the best overviews of the US Army in the ETO.

WARGAMING OPERATIONS IN LORRAINE 1944

The campaign in Lorraine offers both a strategic situation for a high-level operational game, and a series of engagements between armored forces with widely differing morale, equipment and tactical doctrine, for a low-level battle game. It has been assumed that readers wishing to wargame this campaign will follow Hitler's original plan of operations, rather than devise and play through different plans which might be suggested by hindsight.

The View From Headquarters: Operational Map Games

If the game organizer wishes the players to take the roles of Army Group, Army or Corps commanders, he must endeavor to recreate their headquarters, devising systems that will provide incoming information about their own forces and those of the enemy, and determine the outcomes of the players' orders. A 'closed' map game, in which separate teams or individual players submit orders, based upon subjective map displays of the strategic situation and intelligence reports, to an umpire or group of umpires who maintain a central, objective campaign map, and resolve movement, logistics, combat and report back to the players, is a tried and tested structure for a successful operational wargame.

This simple structure can be adapted to most levels of the chain of command, by adjusting the volume and detail of incoming information, both from above and below, and giving players appropriate pre-game briefings. In the case of Manteuffel, this briefing could take the form of a recreation of the meeting on 5 September 1944 with Hitler, role-played by the game organizer or an umpire, who would explain the objectives of the counteroffensive and the forces available to him.

The World War II general's perspective is, in terms of his surroundings and equipment, relatively simple to recreate using large-scale maps upon which intentions and intelligence can be marked; numerous paper documents, ranging from detailed orders of battle and personal files on his subordinate commanders, to current intelligence reports. Two aspects of life at headquarters are, however, much harder to recreate. The first is the sheer volume and depth of intelligence concerning both one's own forces and enemy formations received each day; the second is the professional training and experience of the general and his staff.

Map Kriegsspiel

A more stylized version of the headquarters game for a smaller number of players, who will portray the various army or corps commanders, can be devised on the assumption that the game organizer or umpire will act as their staffs, filtering out irrelevant or unreliable information, summarizing combat and intelligence reports to present them with an

At least three of the Panther tanks participating in the Lorraine fighting have survived, including this Panther Ausf. G preserved at the French tank museum at Saumur. It was captured from Pz. Brig. 112 during the fighting with the French 2nd Armored Division at Dompaire. (Hilary Doyle)

appropriate appreciation of the current situation. An umpire moves formations according to the players' orders, resolves combat, determines expenditure of ammunition and fuel to update the logistic situation, and reports back in accordance with the degree of accuracy appropriate to each side's communication systems. Some attempt should be made to reflect the command styles of individual generals—Patton, for example, insisted upon visiting forward areas to show himself to the troops and assuage his sense of guilt at not sharing the danger of combat.

Each player must specify how his character's time will be spent during the next 24 hours, either by placing counters, labeled "Write Orders", "Inspect Troops", "Reconnaissance", "Dinner" and "Sleep", for example, at the appropriate times of day, or by writing his actions in on a copy of the day track. Should some unforeseen event, or the arrival of fresh intelligence, require him to react, then he may change his plans for the remainder of the day (but not what he has already done), before the umpire judges he would have become aware of the situation. Less experienced or inadequate staffs, such as those of the panzer brigades, will process information more slowly, so there will be a greater delay between events and intelligence of them reaching the general, than will be the case in an efficiently run, experienced headquarters.

The combat results table is governed by the points awarded for ammunition and fuel usage. The average of the ammunition and fuel points could determine the combat effectiveness of an armored formation in attack; but the ammunition points alone represented the strength of a unit engaged in static defense.

Each turn, obviously, represents one day. The game could be played in scaled-down time with all players present, perhaps in different rooms of the game organizer's home, while the umpire updated a master map on the dining table. Alternatively, players could telephone or e-mail their initial orders and actions for the next game-day to the umpire early each evening, and receive situation reports and intelligence later that night, where there would have been time to react that day in reality, or wait until their return home the following day for the situation at the close of that game-day.

"Back-to-Back" Wargames

In a "closed" game structure, using duplicate miniature terrain displays and forces, the players move small-scale troops, vehicles and tanks of their own side on their individual displays. An umpire resolves questions of visibility, calculates the effects of artillery, tank and small-arms fire, and updates both displays by placing upon them only that which would, in reality, be visible, or known by radio communication, to the players' respective characters. This has been called "back-to-back" wargaming, because such a seating arrangement, around the umpire's central model or map, prevents players observing each other's displays. It would, for example, be possible to represent GTL Langlade, or one of its battle-groups, and I/Pz. Regt. 29 quite cheaply for a scenario based upon the action at Dompaire on 13 September.

A multi-player variant of this style of game has been devised by Andy Grainger, in which players take the roles of individual M4 Sherman tank troop commanders, communicating out loud with their own tanks, and with the squadron commander. Each player has a separate table, with a simple model of the terrain immediately around his own tanks, which is updated by one of a team of umpires, who also control the pre-programmed German opposition. This could be adapted very easily to portray the French perspective at Dompaire, or that of the Americans at Arracourt.

Another option is for a group of players to portray the individual members of the crew of one tank — M4, PzKpfw. IV or Panther. The game organizer provides precise details of the crew numbers, their responsibilities in combat, the amount and type of ammunition carried on board, and a plan of the interior of the tank, showing stowage and escape hatches. Those in the turret sit on stools, or a stack of several chairs, so that they are above the driver and other crew members in the hull of the tank, who sit immediately in front of them, facing a detailed miniature terrain, scaled to 15mm, 20mm or 25mm model figures, upon which is a model – probably constructed from an Airfix, or similar, plastic kit – of their own tank, and easily identifiable as such. The driver has a set of "flash cards", one or more of which he displays at each turn to indicate how he is controlling the tank; the gunner and/or loader have a set to show what type of ammunition is being used and a "Fire!" card; the tank commander has cards listing his duties and possible personal actions, but must communicate with his crew only by speech and physical prompts, such as poking the driver's right shoulder to steer right, and so on.

Ideally, all tank crew should wear personal stereos, playing deafening music (unless the game organizer is prepared to go to the trouble of preparing tape recordings of suitable engines) to recreate the effect of motor noise within the crew compartment. Players could also wear cardboard "spectacles", with narrow slits to simulate the view through a periscope or vision port, when the tank's hatch covers are closed, removing them only when they put their heads up through open hatches, thus obtaining a better view of the terrain, but risking being hit by shrapnel or small-arms fire.

Each turn, the players display the appropriate flash cards to indicate their actions. An umpire moves the model of their tank accordingly, resolves questions of visibility and fire, using very simple rules to maintain the speed and tension of play, and gives the players feedback on the situation as necessary. Should their tank be hit, and the commander give the order to bale out, those in the turret must take it in turns to climb upon the commander's stool and jump off, while those inside the hull exit via their own hatches by standing on, and then jumping off, their own chairs – unless the umpire announces that a hatch cover has jammed, when they must exit by an alternative route. Crew members who fail to leave the tank within a specified time will be deemed to have been killed. Several tanks on the same side can participate in this type of game, provided there is an umpire familiar with the rules to monitor each tank. The enemy is best pre-programmed, or controlled by another umpire, whose objective is not to "win" as such, but to provide a realistic and enjoyable game for the players.

Airstrike Game

To conclude, here is an outline for a game to recreate the perspectives of the TALO and the pilots of P-47 Thunderbolt fighter-bombers. The TALO player is equipped with a detailed map of an appropriate area, a pair of toy binoculars, and a cheap intercom. He sits so that his chosen vantage point on a 1/300 groundscale model terrain display, placed several feet away, is at eye level. The P-47 pilot players wait in an adjoining room, with a copy of the same map, individual model 1/144 or 1/72 scale airplanes, some plastic beads and the other intercom.

Each turn, representing about a minute, the TALO player must turn his back to the display while an umpire moves 1/300 German vehicles across the model terrain, and places cotton-wool "shellbursts" to indicate enemy and friendly fire. When the umpire announces that he has finished moving, the TALO player may then turn to face the model and has one minute to decide whether it is necessary to call down an airstrike in real time and, if so, to estimate the grid reference on his map. If he decides to call in an airstrike, he turns away from the table while he communicates with the pilots via the intercom and the umpire times his call and updates the model accordingly; if not, he simply turns away and the umpire advances the enemy the distance they would travel in another minute.

When an airstrike is called down, the first pilot enters the room holding his model plane and gripping a number of small plastic beads or counters to represent the number of bombs carried. He releases his "bombs" when he considers he is on target over the terrain model. The exact height above the model to which he is allowed to dive must be calculated with reference to the vehicle and groundscale. The umpire will throw dice to discover if the airplane is hit by any anti-aircraft fire and the effect of any such hits, informing the pilot orally. The pilot may shout radio messages to his comrades in the adjoining room, and may also receive oral communications from the TALO. When the pilot has dropped his bombs he must leave the room. The TALO player must then turn away while the umpire studies the fall of the plastic beads to discover whether any enemy vehicles have been hit, placing cotton wool bomb bursts as necessary on the model, and advancing the display by the time the pilot was in the room.

The other pilots take it in turn to bomb the target, and the TALO has one last chance to look at the model. After the airstrike, all players whose characters have survived are invited to write individual reports of the mission, estimating enemy losses, which are read aloud before the umpire reveals the true situation on the model. Awards can be made to pilots who scored hits on German vehicles.

Such a game could be combined with a "back-to-back" tank combat game, in which case the player commanding the American or French forces would act as the TALO, or with the tank crew game to give the players of German tank crews an unpleasant shock.

WITHDRAWN

COMPANION SERIES FROM OSPREY

MEN-AT-ARMS
An unrivalled source of information on the organisation, uniforms and equipment of the world's fighting men, past and present. The series covers hundreds of subjects spanning 5,000 years of history. Each 48-page book includes concise texts packed with specific information, some 40 photos, maps and diagrams, and eight colour plates of uniformed figures.

ELITE
Detailed information on the uniforms and insignia of the world's most famous military forces. Each 64-page book contains some 50 photographs and diagrams, and 12 pages of full-colour artwork.

NEW VANGUARD
Comprehensive histories of the design, development and operational use of the world's armoured vehicles and artillery. Each 48-page book contains eight pages of full-colour artwork including a detailed cutaway.

WARRIOR
Definitive analysis of the armour, weapons, tactics and motivation of the fighting men of history. Each 64-page book contains cutaways and exploded artwork of the warrior's weapons and armour.

ORDER OF BATTLE
The most detailed information ever published on the units which fought history's great battles. Each 96-page book contains comprehensive organisation diagrams supported by ultra-detailed colour maps. Each title also includes a large fold-out base map.

AIRCRAFT OF THE ACES
Focuses exclusively on the elite pilots of major air campaigns, and includes unique interviews with surviving aces sourced specifically for each volume. Each 96-page volume contains up to 40 specially commissioned artworks, unit listings, new scale plans and the best archival photography available.

COMBAT AIRCRAFT
Technical information from the world's leading aviation writers on the aircraft types flown. Each 96-page volume contains up to 40 specially commissioned artworks, unit listings, new scale plans and the best archival photography available.